RETIRE

RESET!

RETIRE RESET!

WHAT YOU NEED TO KNOW
AND YOUR FINANCIAL ADVISOR
MAY NOT BE TELLING YOU

M. Nahum Daniels
CFP™ RICP®

Published by Best Seller Publishing, Pasadena, California
Best Seller Publishing® is a registered trademark

ISBN 978-1-946978-77-6

Most Best Seller Publishing® titles are available at special quantity discounts for bulk purchases for sales promotions, premiums, fundraising and educational use. Special versions or book excerpts can also be created to fit specific needs. For more information please write:

Best Seller Publishing®
1346 Walnut Street #205
Pasadena, CA 91106
Or call (626) 765-9750
www.BestSellerPublishing.org

Cover Design: Jon Krackehl
Graphics: Nick Cairl
Layout: Marianne Carroll
Printed in the United States of America

For Tracy

Don't let
the blessings of longevity turn into a curse,
financial repression get you down
or uncertainty keep you up.

Table of Contents

Acknowledgements

Writing this book has required total immersion for going on a year. That concentration has cost me precious time with family, friends and clients and I am grateful to them for the patience they have shown and the emotional support they've offered throughout the process.

I am especially grateful for the critical insight, knowledge and experience contributed by my colleague Dan Slater, a Fellow of the Society of Actuaries and Member of the American Academy of Actuaries. An award-winning product actuary at the epicenter of modern insurance innovation, Dan's vision imbues this work with unparalleled expertise and professional integrity. Any errors in transmission are solely my own.

Randy Randall and Kristi Irving reviewed every version of the manuscript to assure full disclosure, balance and fairness. To the extent that I've achieved these goals, it is due to their commitment to craft.

My interlocutor Matthew Schnarr got me started; my editor Dan Romanowitz worked tirelessly as we strove together for readability and style. From his perch in London, my friend Richard Koppel critiqued an early version of the manuscript bringing to it his unforgiving demands for accuracy and intellectual honesty. My heartfelt thanks go to Nick Cairl whose painstaking work on each figure we've pictured adds thousands of words to the argument.

Finally, my wife, Tracy, both endured my yearlong distraction and applied her experienced developmental eye to the finished product. If it engages you, it's largely thanks to her.

Preface

HOW TO PROFIT FROM THIS BOOK

Learn how to see.

Leonardo da Vinci
Renaissance Artist & Lifetime Learner

D ear Reader,

I wrote this book because I'm a teacher at heart and very important findings in retirement income research have recently come to light. I believe you need to know about them, especially if you're counted among the fortunate 15% of baby boomers with nest eggs of $500,000 or more. Provided they get the proper care and tending, nest eggs of that size offer the potential for an independent, financially secure, and worry-free retirement. Smaller nest eggs need tending all the more.

The findings that I am going to share with you challenge conventional thinking about the financial dynamics that determine retirement success. In professional circles, retirement success is defined simply as not outliving your savings.

My goal is to help you understand some of the key flaws in the investment narrative, helping you explore some unexamined assumptions about the role of stocks and bonds in your portfolio that, in the end, could actually undermine your retirement security. I also aim to illustrate why your expectations about the potential role of insurance may be outdated. In the process, I hope to assist you in reframing your perception of today's economic realities and re-balancing your perspective on how best to navigate retirement's surprising twists and turns. A successful retirement plan requires this mental reset.

But all this requires learning. This book serves as a "how-to" in its last chapters, but its first few are dedicated to setting the stage for today's economic and retirement landscape. I feel that it is imperative to understand and learn from history – both good and bad – to make the most informed (and most important) life decisions. My theory is that understanding the rationale informing my recommendations will motivate you to make the changes to your current arrangements necessary to enhance your odds of achieving retirement success.

Fundamentally, my strategy is built on combining insurance and securities in suitable proportions to complement each other in the service of achieving your financial objectives. What I call my "stable-core" retirement portfolio is anchored to a relatively new insurance contract that I'm convinced is a breakthrough retirement tool that blends some of the most dependable characteristics of insurance together with some of the upside potential of securities. While gaining increasing acceptance in the financial advisory community, it is still widely unknown, so a great deal of this book is dedicated to introducing its concepts and evaluating its strengths and weaknesses along with its possible fit in your portfolio.

I am not the only one in my profession who believes that integrating insurance and securities is at the forefront of contemporary retirement portfolio theory. But I am not yet in the majority. Your current or prospective advisor may or may not have the specialized training in both insurance and securities that full-fledged "retirement-income planning" demands today. To help you determine their preparedness, I've included a total of over 50 essential questions you can ask them. These questions are intended to guide you in conducting the due diligence needed to measure an advisor's true qualifications.

M. Nahum Daniels, CFP™ RICP®
Stamford, Connecticut
New Year's Day 2018

Introduction

FINDING YOUR BALANCE

What financial advisors should acknowledge is the immense impact

that shifting market conditions, longer life expectancies,

and uncertainties surrounding the future of Social Security

have made on our US economy...and the potential of these conditions

to result in a perfect storm...

Roger G. Ibbotson, PhD
Professor Emeritus of Finance, Yale School of Management

Whether you consider it a well-deserved reward for a lifetime of work or a liberating escape from unsatisfying employment, if you're like most Americans you may be obsessed with the idea of retirement. I know many people who can't wait to get started.

But the reality is that most members of the older generation today – the 76-million-strong age cohort born between 1946 and 1964 known as "baby boomers" – simply haven't saved enough. According to a 2016 Price Waterhouse Coopers (PWC) survey, over a third of baby boomers have saved less than $50,000, and of those, most have saved nothing; another 13% have accumulated less than $100,000. Add up the numbers and it becomes clear that half of all baby boomers have less than $100,000 saved for a retirement that could last decades. Only 15% reported nest eggs north of $500,000. We shouldn't be surprised, therefore, by the Social Security Administration's 2017 report that 43% of retired singles and 21% of retired couples count on Social Security for 90% or more of their day-to-day living expenses. Clearly that's a lot of pressure on our social safety net, and that pressure is growing relentlessly as 10,000 boomers enter retirement every day.

By 2030, as many as 76 million members of this one age cohort – almost 20% of our nation's population – will have reached retirement age, collecting their social security benefits and drawing down their retirement savings in an attempt to maintain the lifestyles (or some semblance of them) to which they've grown accustomed. Given dramatic improvements in longevity, modern retirement could extend 30 years or more, which is a very long time to make money last, especially when it may be earning very little. The bottom line? Americans without savings or with very little will not be able to stop working without material compromise pretty much as soon as retirement begins. But even those who may have enough at the outset face the risk of losses that could impose compromises later. And that can be true regardless of how much money you start with if you ignore today's rules and ratios as applied to retirement income planning, and/or simply run into bad luck.

Which brings us to what this book offers: an investment strategy for individuals with the wherewithal, willingness, and desire to accept personal responsibility for their financial independence in retirement. My approach is intended to help insulate your nest egg from crippling losses while enabling you to grow it and your income in good markets and bad. What I have found over a long career as a financial advisor is that many baby boomers lack the mindset and tactics to optimally leverage their wealth as they transition into and navigate retirement.

This book is intended to address that shortcoming by showing you how to construct what I call the "stable core" retirement portfolio. It's a portfolio designed to withstand worst-case market scenarios while positioning you to participate in positive market outcomes. It's income-focused and strives for simplicity as its primary objective. And it aspires to add even more value to your life by protecting you from some of your worst instincts (like buying high and selling low), freeing you from some of your worst fears (like running out of money), and in the end (i.e., during those golden years) enabling you to live generously, unafraid to share your good fortune with the people and causes you care about.

I've spent my career as a financial advisor testing this portfolio, observing its behavior under different market conditions, and comparing its performance to the alternatives. During the development process I continuously searched for different ideas and approaches to retirement portfolio construction. Trained in a broad range of investment methodologies and money management styles, I came to the discovery phase with no specific expectations. In fact, I like to think I brought a "Zen mind" to my quest, a non-judgmental beginner's openness I first learned about as a young man living in Japan in the 1970s. I also brought a desire for simplicity, in the mold of the ancient Taoists who reduced all phenomena to an inter-play of only two antagonistic but complementary energies, the yin and the yang. These two cosmic forces form an integrated whole expressed in the myriad cycles of nature—and they infuse the financial world just as they do all other areas of life.

After decades of professional practice, it has become clear to me that in terms of retirement planning, the conventional mindset falls short. For starters, no matter how well it may have served you in earlier lifecycle phases, the traditional thinking simply doesn't prepare you for what you're up against. That's because the challenges unique to retirement are not encountered in earlier phases of our financial lives; we don't confront them until we are face-to-face, often with inadequate preparation and sometimes leading to irrecoverable losses. As we will find later on, losses can ruin even the best-laid plan.

In fact, financial success in earlier phases of life often ingrains investment concepts, expectations and biases that are actually contraindicated in retirement. These include some of the most fundamental precepts that underpin investment and retirement practice today, such as the importance of asset selection and portfolio balance, sustainable withdrawal rates and probability analysis. Among these ingrained biases, the most dangerous are complacency and overconfidence. Granted, optimism has its place in healthy human psychology, but it should not be a guiding principle in your retirement planning. Optimism in retirement planning simply isn't prudent. I recommend that in ideal planning, a healthy wariness of the unknown should be cultivated.

Today, baby boomers are constantly bombarded with pitches emanating from the two poles of the money management industry. In my yin and yang vernacular, I call these poles "banking" and "insurance" and I intend to demonstrate that they are diametric opposites when it comes to retirement strategy and tactics. Put simply, the banking sector originates and transmits risk, and the insurance sector mitigates and absorbs it. I believe that for best results they need to be integrated, weighted properly to serve your specific retirement needs and objectives. The reality is, however, that few advisors are versed in both disciplines, reflecting an-all-too common training imbalance that regularly reveals itself through skewed results.

In both academic circles and on the street, these two schools of thought compete for theoretical leadership and market dominance.

Members of the banking school are trained to favor securities. They recommend that retirement-focused investors expose their portfolios to stocks and bonds if they wish to earn total returns sufficient to pace their retirement income with long-term inflation and have something left over for heirs. They champion risk assets even though it may mean bearing ill-timed capital losses, confident in the belief that those losses will almost always be recoverable and simply must be endured as an inescapable aspect of the investment process. Advisors trained in this discipline tend to be relatively uninformed about insurance products and actuarial science, often relegating both to a background role in retirement portfolio construction, if they give them any role at all.

Advocates of the insurance school emphasize guarantees over returns, putting loss avoidance and safety of principal first, with focus on the intrinsic value of lifelong cash flow. But the cash flow paid out by the traditional annuity contract used for this purpose is almost always fixed, i.e., paid in the form of an unchanging paycheck year in and year out. Over time, a fixed income suffers serious purchasing-power erosion due to inflationary public policy and an ever-rising cost of living. Financial advisors principally trained in the insurance school may themselves defer to the preeminence of securities in the retirement portfolio, surrendering to today's mainstream "retirement investing" narrative.

Ironically, I've found that most practitioners of these two interrelated schools barely speak each other's language. Securities-centric advisors are focused on wealth accumulation; hence retirement planning comes to mean adapting the tactics of accumulation to spin off income. Insurance-centric advisors tend to be focused on risk management and are reluctant to apply the language of investing to the traditional insurance products they recommend primarily for a fixed, albeit guaranteed, yield.

But what I've learned over many years of practice is that retirees are not just "older investors" who need to merely readjust the ratio of stocks, bonds, and cash in their portfolios (one formula calls for subtracting your age from 100 to determine the proportion of bonds appropriate for your stage of life). Retirees are fragile. They have very little tolerance for loss (even if they think they do) or capacity for it (even if they have accumulated a considerable store of wealth) because they just don't have enough time to recover from financial setbacks. Meanwhile, they may actually have too much time on this earth—more than they ever thought possible—and need to plan for what could be a lifespan exceeding 95 years, with each one of those years accompanied by a rise in the cost of living. Given a 3% average rate of inflation, the purchasing power of a fixed income will suffer proportionately.

Retirement is filled with such unexpected paradoxes, challenging you to balance too little and too much of the very same thing decades in advance. Modern retirement planning is a relatively new field that seeks to anticipate those surprising twists and turns not encountered in earlier phases of our lives. It has emerged over the last twenty years to serve baby boomer demand as 76 million people shape this new phase of their lives—and our nation's—relatively unprepared but naively confident, according to the findings of countless retirement industry surveys.

Centered around financial planning, retirement advice extends beyond conventional portfolio management to include issues of life and death, health and wellness, disability and infirmity, even food and shelter, all of which impact the investment portfolio and must be taken into account when wealth is allocated specifically toward generating long-term income. The reality is that while retirement success encompasses investment success, it also transcends it. Measured quantitatively, investment success is defined as generating returns that outperform a stock market index by enough to justify any additional risk assumed to do it, and achieving that success may earn you boasting rights in a golf club locker room. Retirement success is far more nuanced. It is grounded in ensuring yourself a paycheck to sustain your desired standard of living for as long as you (and your spouse) may live while freeing you from financial anxiety and self-denial. It should be measured qualitatively when you look back and determine whether you've run the race and won.

Thus, while investment management can be done at arm's length, retirement planning gets very personal, calling upon a different professional skill set. Training is essential. Experience is invaluable. A holistic orientation verging on "life coaching" can be helpful, further distinguishing the field from Artificial Intelligence-generated robo-advisory services. The robo-advisor epitomizes a mechanical approach that ignores actuarial intelligence. It is built on the policy portfolio and Modern Portfolio Theory (MPT) and is destined to fail to deliver that paycheck because it doesn't address the complex risks unique to retirement. Indeed, Professor Harry Markowitz, MPT's Nobel Prize-winning developer, has himself made clear that his portfolio theory was never intended to guide people's retirement asset management.

The risks unique to retirement—amplified by today's economic uncertainties—must stay uppermost in your mind and your advisor's. To succeed, it's imperative that you define and acknowledge them, then design a retirement portfolio that can withstand whatever is thrown at you and even turn adversity into opportunity. In other words, as a modern retiree, your first task is to hedge, literally anchoring your nest egg—the money you've saved specifically to fund your retirement—to the most efficient hedges(s) you can find or bear the consequences.

My purpose in writing this book is to prepare you for the money management challenges you will encounter as you approach, enter, and navigate retirement and to guide you in balancing these two contending forces—banking and insurance—that battle to shape your retirement worldview and practical tactics. Trained in both the language of investing and the language of insurance, I want to show you how you can integrate your approach by investing your savings in an innovative financial hybrid—combining some features of securities with some features of insurance—ingeniously engineered to anchor a retirement portfolio. It's known as the Fixed Index Annuity (FIA) and I'm convinced it's a game-changing product for retirees and contemporary retirement planning.

The FIA is an insured retirement contract designed to protect your nest egg from market losses, position it to capture a share of market gains and increase the guaranteed income it can stream when you convert it into a series of paychecks that go on as long you do.

Notwithstanding its limitations (including early inaccessibility without surrender charges, limitations on how much of the market upside you can capture, withdrawals taxed as ordinary income, and others addressed throughout this book) understanding how the FIA may fit at the heart of your portfolio can enhance your odds of retirement success, helping you to sustain your desired standard of living even in the face of adverse markets.

The goal of this book is to show you how and why the FIA may serve as an efficient hedge that can help you meet your retirement objectives. Once your nest egg is weighted appropriately to the FIA, any remaining assets can be considered "surplus" available for allocation to riskier asset classes. Playing an important supporting role, risk assets may also have a place in your retirement portfolio. Which risk assets you choose and how big an allocation you make to them will depend on your specific needs, goals, resources, and appetite.

Your financial advisor should provide you an evaluation of the FIA and its possible fit in your retirement asset mix. This book is intended to prepare you to engage knowledgeably, regardless of which language your advisor may speak.

As a Certified Financial Planner™ practitioner, I have been a fiduciary almost since first entering the planning profession over thirty years ago. As a fiduciary, my legal and ethical duty is to always put your interests before my own as I endeavor to help you see where your true interests really lie. As we embark together on this journey, I promise to stay true to my duty. In turn, I ask you to travel this path with a Zen mind, open to learning new things and to seeing the world and your choices differently. I believe that effective retirement planning in fact starts with this shift in your gestalt.

Takeaways

1. The FIA is an investment-oriented insurance contract that guarantees a lifetime of income offering growth potential, but also has a number of offsetting limitations detailed in the End Notes of this book and discussed throughout it, which should be weighed thoughtfully before you invest.

2. Two antagonistic schools of thought set the parameters of retirement planning today and offer very different approaches to managing the risks encountered in the retirement process. For a detailed comparison of the two, cf. Appendix 1.

3. Every nest egg needs to find its unique balance of these two approaches—as embodied in the allocation tactics they advocate—to maximize the odds of retirement success.

4. Retirees are not just older investors; they are fragile and lack the time needed to recover from financial setbacks.

5. Most traditional insurance contracts pay fixed income streams for a specific number of years (or for life) that are likely to lag inflation.

Questions for your financial advisor

1. How much training in retirement planning, as distinct from investment and/or insurance planning, have you had and do you hold any professional designations in the field?

2. How much of your practice is dedicated to retirement planning; do you specialize in it or is it incidental to a more diversified set of investment or insurance services you offer?

3. Do you offer the FIA to clients preparing for, entering or already in retirement?

4. If you do, what do you understand to be its role, and do you treat it as peripheral or central to portfolio construction?

5. If you don't offer the FIA as an investment alternative, why don't you?

be

the

last

winner

Michio Kushi

1926-2014

Chapter 1

DEMOGRAPHICS ARE DESTINY

Today we are living through a profound shift in demography…

contributing to two of the defining characteristics of the

current economic environment: slow growth and low interest rates.

Bruce Wolfe, CFA and Russ Koesterich, CFA
BlackRock Retirement Institute

One evening not long ago I broke bread with a 55-year-old friend whose age placed him at the tail end of the baby boom generation. Most people would have considered his situation enviable—the father of three gifted teenage boys, married to a talented artist, living in a beautiful home in an affluent suburb of New York City. He had officially retired ten years earlier from a stressful but successful career working for one of Wall Street's most prominent firms. The decade he had spent as an investment banker left him with a respectable portfolio to manage. He had done so since his early retirement with considerable success, although the level of stock market risk he perceived during the past few years had deterred him from participating, resulting in a few flat years; alas, home improvements continued apace together with private school tuitions.

As we were catching up on world events, this very worldly man leaned over and informed me that upon reassessment of his overall finances—in view of soon having to pony up $1 million or so for (hopefully) three Ivy League educations—he had decided never to buy himself another pair of shoes. After all, he explained, he had spent top dollar on the shoes he collected during his active career years; buying only the best that Europe had to offer, he had always taken conscientious care of them and always would. And he expected their craftsmanship to hold up for as long as he might live, maybe forty more years if he followed in his 95-year-old father's footsteps. And there he left it, moving on to European politics.

I have pondered his declaration of early-stage self-denial ever since that evening. Unpacked, it reveals the predicament of a generation of Americans facing unprecedented economic challenges almost no matter the level of financial wherewithal they may enjoy. My friend didn't couch his conclusion in economic theory or market analytics. He articulated it as a simple matter of fact emanating from his deepest financial instincts. Effectively retired and looking ahead, he was facing the reality of making trade-offs in his quality of life far earlier than he would have ever thought. His response to the prospect of a forty-year future without employment income and the anxiety it provoked in the face of economic uncertainty was to tighten his belt a notch for the first time, despite his membership in America's top 0.10% high net worth fraternity.

Many Americans today share his anxiety confronting retirement. As a retirement advisor, I've come to know it well. I focus on its financial dynamics. I'm not a lifestyle coach or a self-realization guru, *per se,* though I am a student of psychology and do aspire to a steady state of wellbeing, and I recognize what the anxiety is all about. In retirement, cash flow is king. If you have more than you need, you have a shot at equanimity and generosity; if you have less, you may find yourself making some difficult compromises.

Is retirement supposed to be a time for self-expression and self-fulfillment after a long working life that required self-discipline and self-sacrifice? You bet it is. But it can be expensive, and you have to be able to pay for it. So you need to reset and, at this point in your life, it's likely your financial beliefs and habits are firmly entrenched. In this chapter, we explore some of the key structural issues that most of us don't think that much about but should, because they directly impact our planning and results.

The Transcendent Issue of the 21st Century

When closely examined, the retirement challenges we face as a society are actually much more complex than they first appear. The mainstream media skate along the surface, pointing to long-lived baby boomers with inadequate personal savings looking to a fragile if not insolvent social security system unable to make up the difference. All true. Upon deeper analysis, though, it turns out there's even more to the problem, including slowing population growth, shrinking consumer demand, exploding debt, inflated financial bubbles in the stock and bond markets, deflationary wage and employment pressures and over-spent governments at odds with their own citizens. Without understanding the surprising connectivity of these global forces it's hard to appreciate the tsunami they may be forming.

The headwinds we face are driven by a sea change in domestic and global "demographics," or the ratio of different age groups in society. With fertility rates falling and longevity rising, the industrialized world is entering an unprecedented era of hyper-aging. As a result of modern medicine and improved hygiene, global life expectancy has improved dramatically over the last 50 years and Americans are living longer than ever before. According to data from the Centers for Disease Control (CDC), average US life expectancy has rocketed from 47 to 79 over the past hundred years. What's more, our fastest growing age groups are the octogenarians and nonagenarians. In its latest report "The Older Population in the United States: 2010-2050" the Census Bureau predicts that over the next three decades the number of people in the U.S. over the age of 65 is expected to double while those 85 and up (the "oldest old") will triple. This may be good news for baby boomers who stay vital, but it's bad news for the survivability of the social safety net.

Of course, living a long, active, self-reliant life into our eighties or nineties can be a blessing, a period of extended contribution and enriched meaning. Two of my most remarkable clients definitely feel that way. They make up a husband and wife team of medical doctors who treat patients, design and oversee innovative research, write books and lead international organizations. He just celebrated his 92nd birthday and she her 90th. They still work full-time and see no reason to pack it in, believing that their work is simply not done.

On the other hand, a long life characterized by infirmity, incapacity, and scarcity after a career of unsatisfying labor can feel like a curse. Whether a blessing or a curse, one thing remains true: longevity costs money. Writing in Foreign Affairs at the end of the

20th Century, economist Peter "Pete" Peterson estimated the looming cost of longevity worldwide to run into the quadrillions.

Magnifying the challenge facing developed countries caused by unprecedented growth in the number of their elderly will be the equally unprecedented decline in the number of their youth. According to UN statistics, the average fertility rate in the world (excluding Africa) has already fallen below 2.1, the rate required to maintain a constant population size. In 2016 the US fertility rate hit a historic low, according to the CDC, falling 1% from 2015, to 62 births per 1,000 women ages 15 to 44. Unless fertility rates in Europe and Japan rebound, their total populations will shrink to about one-half their current size by the end of this century, reducing the ratio of working taxpayers to nonworking pensioners to as low as 1:1 by 2050. How governments and societies come to terms with their shrinking populations in an aging world will become, in Peterson's words, "the transcendent economic issue of the 21st Century."

Baby Boomers Are the Leading Edge

By virtue of its sheer numbers, cultural influence and economic impact, the baby boom generation has exerted an outsized influence on American life at every stage of its evolution. Sure enough, the boomers are doing it again as they enter their retirement phase under-saved and unabashed at making trillion-dollar demands on our government and economy at a time when both are stressed and ill prepared to meet them. This is not to suggest for a moment that—after faithfully contributing to the Social Security trust fund for decades—they're not entitled.

But while long-lived baby boomers are at the forefront of the retirement avalanche, the predicament facing the millennial generation (born between 1983 and 2001) exacerbates the situation. While it's been commonly assumed that each American generation would do better than the previous one, this is not necessarily the case for the millennials. While they number 75 million, their income earning potential is down from previous generations, and neither their economic circumstances nor their prospects are nearly as promising. Unable to jumpstart high-paying careers in a sluggish economy, many millennials are disproportionately debt-burdened, low-wage-earning, living at home, slow at independent household formation and delaying child bearing. According to the CDC study, it was primarily millennials' declining fertility in 2017 that dragged the nation's overall rate down to 1.88, i.e., below the replacement rate of 2.1. Unless their economic circumstances change, they simply cannot be counted on to grow consumption or ascend to high-paying jobs to mature into productive taxpayers, social security contributors and reproductive mates.

At the same time, we cannot close our eyes to our nation's soft middle. Between the 76 million retiring baby boomers slowing their consumption at one end of the continuum and the 75 million millennials unemployed or underemployed struggling to gain economic traction at the other end, reside 10 million prime working age American males ages 25 to 54 who have dropped out of the workforce entirely. Poignantly described by Nicholas Eberstadt in his 2016 book "Men Without Work," these predominantly high-school educated white males are not just unemployed; they've given up and are not looking. Because they are not participating, they aren't counted in official unemployment statistics. According to the Census

Bureau's Survey of Income and Program Participation, as of 2013, around 50% of this group collects social security disability benefits (SSDI), which drains the retirement system's reserves and also makes the recipients eligible for Medicaid. With Medicaid come cheap narcotics. As a result, according to Princeton University economist Alan Krueger writing in a 2017 Brookings Institute study, nearly half of the men who dropped out of the workforce are estimated to be on opioid painkillers. Eberstadt, too, laments that opioid addiction has become rampant among 50-something white working-class men in America and that "deaths of despair" from suicide, alcoholism and drug overdoses are now epidemic within this group. Based on research conducted by demographer Sarah Shannon and others, Eberstadt further calculates that as of the end of 2016, at least another 20 million-or-so working-age men are convicted felons. With approximately 10% incarcerated at any one time, that leaves perhaps 18 million or more looking for work but largely unemployable because of the stigma they carry. Altogether, these groups of unemployed and unemployable working-age men form an "invisible crisis," warns Eberstadt, creating a disruptive demographic force that further depresses consumptive demand.

We are a Nation of Consumers

In our economy, aggregate consumer demand is an elemental force. We are a nation of consumers. According to the Bureau of Economic Analysis, the research arm of the U.S. Department of Commerce, almost 70% of our annual gross domestic product (GDP)—the retail value of all economic transactions—reflects consumer demand, the desire to buy products and services combined with the willingness and ability to pay for them. Americans adopted the consumption ethos in the Roaring Twenties when, after climbing out of a short-lived but steep depression between 1920-1922, we were sold on improving our everyday lives with the technological breakthroughs that promised a higher standard of living, like telephones, refrigerators, washing machines, irons, radios and, above all, automobiles. Broad consumer demand generated a virtuous cycle of economic growth, job creation, and income and productivity improvements that all added up to a bigger economic pie.

Economist and author Harry Dent argues that in every generation workers aged 45-55 exert a defining impact on national consumption as they fund their "peak-spending wave." Entering their highest earning years, this age cohort tends to generate huge demand for housing, furnishings, SUVs, children's educations and all the other staples of affluent American life. Before riding their peak-spending wave they build up their earnings; after the wave they reduce demand to save up for retirement. Dent argues that timing each generation's spending wave provides economic predictive power because consumptive demand—whether *current* derived from today's earning power, *pent-up* reflecting delayed consumption, or *pulled forward* from future earnings in the form of debt—drives the pace and direction of economic activity here and throughout the industrialized world.

That's why the economic importance of a growing, childbearing middle class cannot be overstated. The closing of thousands of factories in the US since the mid-1990s and the loss of millions of relatively high-paying manufacturing jobs, coupled with the nine million more lost during the Great Recession that followed the Global Financial Crisis of 2008 (GFC) has, by all accounts, hollowed out the middle-class. Low wages and unemployment are presenting young Americans with an existential crisis. According to the Census Bureau, in 2016 the US population grew at the slowest pace since the Great Depression, largely driven by a collapse in household formation as the number of millennials living with their parents hit 34%, a 75-year high. Economist Lacy Hunt has pointed out that from 2006-2016, real per capita disposable income rose by only 1%, less than half the fifty-year average, while the 2017 Department of Agriculture report "Expenditures on Children by Families" shows that the nationwide after-tax average cost of raising a child born in 2015 ranges from $175,000 to $375,000 through age 17 (not including a college education). No wonder many millennials may be put off by the prospect of child rearing. In the words of demographer Chris Hamilton, we are facing a "birth dearth," with the number of American children ages 0-4, headwaters of US growth, stalled at just under 20 million since 2005.

Secular Stagnation

Thanks in large measure to former Harvard University President, former US Treasury Secretary and current Harvard economics professor Lawrence Summers, recognition of the defining influence of demographics on our economic wellbeing is coming into academic vogue. Since delivering a seminal presentation to the International Monetary Fund (IMF) in 2013, Summers has become perhaps the leading proponent of the "secular stagnation" theory to explain why America's economy has lagged even the most pessimistic predictions for recovery from the Great Recession—and why it might never recover its former dynamism without a huge dose of government stimulus, if even then.

According to the Bureau of Economic Analysis, the reality is that for nearly a decade as of this writing, the economy has struggled to achieve 1.5% annual growth – despite the infusion of at least $4 trillion in Federal Reserve fiat money into the banking system and another $9 trillion borrowed and spent by the federal government. Since 2000 GDP growth has been persistently low, averaging about 2 percent, while between 1970 and 2000 GDP growth averaged above 3 percent and some years saw even more. This lagging growth rate confounds conventional economic theories. Professor Summers' proposed explanation is controversial: our current slow growth, he says, is not a result of the ups and downs of the "normal" business cycle or of mistaken government fiscal or regulatory policies, but reflects a much different economic condition. It's characterized as a state of "secular stagnation"—a long-term (i.e., secular) sustained (i.e., non-cyclical) paralysis in economic development caused by the adverse demographic changes described by the age wave—accompanied by a dearth of major technological innovation on the scale of the personal computer and Internet.

While often ascribed to be the thought leader in this emerging school of economic analysis, Professor Summers did not originate the theory of demographics-driven secular stagnation. It was first proposed by Harvard economist Alvin Hansen in 1938 to explain the sluggish recovery that followed the Great Depression. Hansen presented his theory at the historic low point of American population growth – just over 0.5% in 1937 – a depressed level that wouldn't be reached again until 2015, some eighty years later. Hansen reasoned that without new people entering the workforce and new inventions coming to market, there would be less business investment. Without investment spending, growth would slow, and more workers would be unable to find jobs in a vicious downward spiral. The baby boom explosion after World War II was therefore just what the US economy needed to reignite growth; the post-war population surge emerged in tandem with the introduction of innumerable new devices, including the computer, which was developed in the war effort. Sure enough, while the standard thinking of the day was that the United States would sink back into a deep depression at the war's end, instead the postwar economy sparked a 30-year period of above average expansion. Despite the occasional business-cycle recession, good times rolled.

But that was then. Today, the baby boom generation finds itself hoping for a normal business-cycle recovery. Unfortunately, nearly a decade since the Global Financial Crisis and the resulting Great Recession that ended in June 2009—the worst economic contraction since the Great Depression—a proven recovery has yet to materialize despite the extraordinary efforts of our central planners at the Fed and in the Treasury Department. The theory of secular stagnation would explain that with too few buyers and too little spending, businesses cut back investment in new factories, workers, and equipment, leading to even fewer jobs for the core working-age population (ages 20-64) and further suppressing demand in an ever-worsening spiral. To quote Hansen's dire conclusion, if this contracting population/employment/spending trend persists for prime working age Americans, precisely when the baby boomers will be retiring and reducing their own personal demand, then baby boomers may be facing the unsettling prospect of "sick recoveries which die in their infancy and depressions which feed on themselves." This could take the form of a grinding slow-growth economy that drags on for decades. Having grown up in times of relative prosperity in the 1980s and 1990s, this is not what baby boomers were raised to expect.

Debt

But did the economic growth of the 1980s and 1990s that accustomed the baby boomers to a prosperous lifestyle qualify as genuine prosperity? The truth is that we may have started living with the economic effects of secular stagnation decades ago, stemming from a demographic tipping point actually reached in 1978. As illustrated in Figure 1, that was the year that the annual rate of US adult population growth reached a post-1967 peak of 1.9% and began to trend down.

FIGURE 1. AN EYE-OPENING CO-INCIDENCE OF PRIMAL ECONOMIC FORCES

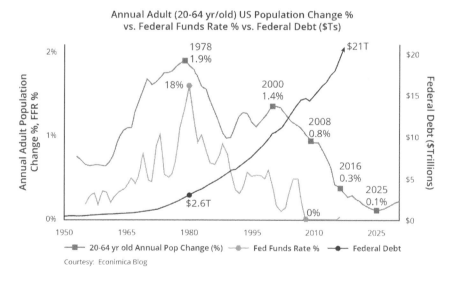

Courtesy: Econimica Blog

We would expect declining demand and slowing economic growth to accompany contracting population growth and, true to form, starting in 1978 the year-over-year growth in US GDP began to trend down, paralleled by a decline in employment and wage growth. So where did this perceived prosperity come from? Demand would have to be pulled forward from the future in the form of debt.

FIGURE 2. RISING HOUSEHOLD DEBT LEVELS HAVE BEEN USED TO OFFSET DECLINING INCOMES AND GDP

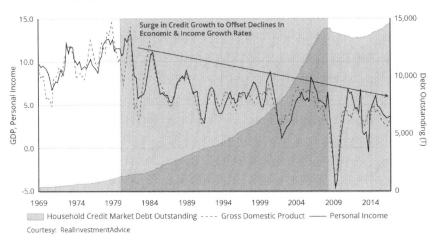

Courtesy: RealInvestmentAdvice

Conveniently, two mutually reinforcing socioeconomic developments unfolded right at this demographic turning point. First, to provide stimulus to a slowing economy, the Reagan administration declared deficit spending thoroughly acceptable (i.e., "deficits don't matter") and US federal debt began its inexorable climb from $900 billion in 1980 to over $21 trillion in 2018. Fortuitously, borrowing got cheaper as the base-setting Fed Funds Rate (FFR) began its long decline from 18% in 1980 to today's roughly one percent. Second, at around the same time, aiming to make up the difference between household income and the cost of living, Americans changed their minds about living beyond their means and started to take on household debt. According to a report issued by the Federal Reserve Bank of New York, household debt has since risen from $790 billion in 1978 to an all-time high of $12.7 trillion in 2017. According to St.

Louis Fed data, total US debt (government, corporate, household) is approaching $65 trillion at the time of this writing, over 3.5 times 2016 GDP. Without all that debt, which drove GDP growth by sustaining both demand and spending power, economic growth would have slowed decades ago.

Ever-increasing corporate, household and federal debt (currently $65 trillion) is a lot to contemplate and a lot to service. Despite historically low rates, debt service—the interest we pay—imposes a huge drag on spending, whether for investment or consumption. The process of debt creation feeds on itself: if the balloon stops expanding, we are told, it might implode, possibly leading to a full-blown economic depression. In fact, the economists and bankers who set central bank policy profess that the only cure to too much debt in the world today is more debt.

Many observers believe that in pursuit of sustainable prosperity, debt creation to feed aggregate demand has also had troubling ancillary effects. According to them, along with propagating income and wealth inequality, the debt creation process serves to motivate speculation and thereby distort financial markets by driving financial asset prices to historic highs that are disconnected from economic fundamentals. Individuals already in ownership of those financial assets get wealthier and people without them get alienated, while stock and bond markets grow riskier. If the debt bubble were to blow, financial asset prices could deflate rapidly. This scenario would undermine retirees who are relying almost entirely on their nest eggs to see them through.

The Nest Egg Ascendant

In the 20th Century, retirees built their retirement cash flows on a foundation of pension promises enhanced by social security benefits and topped off by their "nest egg"--their personal savings earmarked for retirement. The pension guaranteed risk-free lifelong payments based on an employer's pension assets specifically set aside and professionally managed to meet maturing obligations. Scheduled social security benefits were also believed to be risk-free and completely dependable, guaranteed by the federal government and paid out by the Social Security Trust Fund from contributions paid into the system by younger participants and backed by the Trust's accumulated surpluses. And finally came the nest egg, which was considered supplemental, intended to top up the other two income sources; because it was supplemental, it might even be exposed to a measure of risk in pursuit of "excess" return.

FIGURE 3. IN THE 21ST CENTURY YOUR NEST EGG WILL SHAPE YOUR RETIREMENT DESTINY

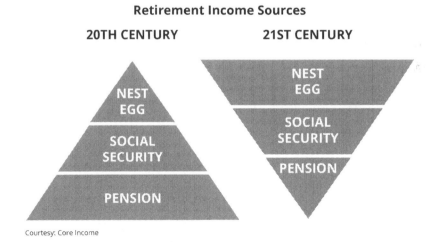

Retirement Income Sources

20TH CENTURY   **21ST CENTURY**

NEST EGG

SOCIAL SECURITY

PENSION

NEST EGG

SOCIAL SECURITY

PENSION

Courtesy: Core Income

Today, as shown in Figure 3, the traditional orientation has been turned on its head. For retirees with assets, the personal nest egg is in fact the cornerstone of any personal retirement income plan; it must be protected and managed for optimum lifelong performance. Though it is helpful while it lasts, the social security benefit flow is secondary because it is limited by formula in amount (according to the Social Security Administration average social security benefits paid in 2017 were $1,360 per month), its future viability is uncertain (the 2017 Trustees Annual Report schedules benefit reductions of at least 25% starting in 2034 when it projects the depletion of the Trust Fund), and any other changes deemed necessary to preserve the system are out of your control. Ironically, pension benefits—public or private—may be the most susceptible to under performance in the years ahead because over-stretched plans may end up at the very center of the next bear market-triggered financial crisis, given how over-exposed they tend to be to stocks.

The traditional organizational pension, or defined benefit (DB) plan, is exceedingly rare today, having been replaced in the 1980s and 1990s by the introduction of the defined contribution plan best known as the 401(k). The DB plan required the sponsoring entity to guarantee a lifetime income benefit to the retired employee based on a formula that multiplied average earnings by years of service. The plan sponsor assumed all the market risk in assuring asset adequacy to meet the plan's legal obligations. DB plans are rare today because they're expensive to administer, costly to fund and risky to take on. In the 401(k) plan, participants make their own contribution from earnings, select from a menu of investments, and are personally responsible for the results.

Whether active or frozen, surviving pension plans still pay out backed up by the Pension Benefit Guarantee Corporation (PBGC). Based on its latest data, the PBGC estimates that as of 2015 the average pension plan was underfunded by at least 50%. The PBGC is a semi-governmental agency which is itself severely undercapitalized at approximately 70% and was reported in 2012 to be two or three major plan failures away from a federal bailout. If and when the reckoning comes, the PBGC will likely oversee equitable benefit reduction rather than full benefit restoration, effectively distributing the pain rather than keeping plan participants whole.

Private pensions are not the only ones with "unfunded liabilities," the lump sum additions needed *today* to meet payout promises *tomorrow* that cannot be met by current plan assets earning expected investment returns. Today, many public-sector pension plans—state, local and union—are also seriously underfunded, and countless public-sector employees and union members are relying on these plans. In April 2016, Moody's credit rating agency used a return assumption of around 4% to calculate the 75-year unfunded liability for all state and local pension plans and pegged the shortfall at $3.5 trillion. Using the same actuarial data but a more conservative Treasury bond return of 2.6%, the American Enterprise Institute calculated the shortfall at $5.2 trillion.

Moody's also quantified the unfunded liabilities of the various federal pension systems covering civilian and military employee benefits. The current shortfall: $3.5 trillion. Unbeknownst to most of their participants, US public pensions address this underfunding by taking on much more investment risk than their European and Asian counterparts. The unpalatable alternatives would be increased participant contributions or reduced participant benefits. But if the numbers are right and the unfunded liabilities are not set aside today (which is unlikely), promised benefits will have to be cut in the future, sometimes by as much as half, or even more.

Cutbacks of this magnitude could have very serious repercussions. Recall that many older pensioners live on very tight budgets focused on necessities like food, housing, healthcare, and transportation. Every $1 held back represents a measure of austerity; think of the personal suffering endured by pensioners reduced to penury in Greece, for example, leading to impaired physical health, psychological distress, personal moral degradation and even suicide. Remember, too, that every $1 in spending removed from the US economy this way will have negative multiplier effects.

But the 2016 report reveals that these numbers pale in the shadow of the unfunded liabilities for the Social Security and Medicare programs. Moody's estimated the Social Security funding gap as of April 2016 at $13.4 trillion and the shortfall from the Hospital Insurance component of the Medicare program (Part B) at $3.2 trillion.

In sum, according to Moody's, the total aging-related funding shortfall at all levels of government as of April 2016 looks like this:

TABLE 1. ESTIMATED GOVERNMENT RETIREE FUNDING SHORTFALLS

Retiree Program	Unfunded Liability (Trillions)
Social Security	$13.4
Medicare Part B	3.2
Federal Pensions	3.5
State & Local Pensions	3.5
Source: Moody's 2016 Survey TOTAL	$23.6 Trillion

If these calculations are correct, $23.6 trillion is the minimum amount that would have to be contributed to these programs *today* to ensure that they can cover their projected payouts over the next 75 years. Where does that money come from? Theoretically from taxpayers, preferably in the form of an increasing number of high-paid younger workers earning growing incomes in an expanding economy. But will those working-age Americans have well-paying jobs in 2050 that will sufficiently support the needed level of FICA contributions? Professor Summers projects that, if secular economic stagnation persists, one out of every five working age males could be unemployed by 2050. That level of unemployment combined with a drop in sheer worker numbers could reduce the effective support ratio – the number of workers per retiree – to much less than 2:1. The effective support ratio dropped to fewer than 3:1 in 2015 after reaching 16:1 in 1950. As a result, in 2016 the system took in $53 billion less in payroll taxes than it paid out to its 50 million beneficiaries, and had to tap into its $2.8 trillion trust fund to make up the shortfall.

FIGURE 4. THE HISTORY AND HEALTH OF SOCIAL SECURITY

Enacted in 1935 with an Original Full Retirement Age (FRA) of 65.

• Life expectancy in 1935 was 60 years, 65.7 years excluding infant mortality

Workers per retiree:

• 1950: 16 to 1
• 2016: 2.8 to 1

$869 Billion
Payroll taxes paid by covered workers in 2016

$2.8 Trillion Trust Fund

$922 Billion
Total expenditures/benefits paid in 2016

Trust Fund Reserves On Track to Deplete by 2035
75% of benefits to be paid starting in 2034

Source: 2017 Social Security Trustees Annual report dated July 13, 2017

The Social Security Trust Fund

Thanks to the highly favorable ratio of workers to retirees in earlier years, the Social Security Trust Fund had regularly generated surpluses and had grown substantially. Unlike a standard insurance reserve or pension plan, however, the Trust Fund was limited by law as to how it could "invest" its accumulating surpluses. Statute required that they had to be used to buy "governmental accounting series" debt, i.e., government bonds that cannot be sold to outside investors on the open market and can only be redeemed at maturity by the US government.

Eventually, the Social Security trust account—funded predominantly by the baby boomers—became the federal government's largest single bond buyer and its predominant creditor. At $2.8 trillion, it's owed more today than is currently owed to China and Japan combined ($2.3 trillion). With no more incoming surplus, the Trust can no longer purchase US government debt; on the contrary, the Treasury has to start paying up, redeeming what the Trust already owns in exchange for cash. The declining support ratio has thus triggered a material change in intergovernmental accounting. Without the Social Security Trust Fund serving as a captive buyer, new debt will have to be sold to new buyers—both foreign and domestic—if they can be found.

When Alvin Hansen first introduced his theory of secular stagnation to the American Economic Association in his presidential address on December 28, 1938, he cautioned that "we are moving swiftly out of the order in which those of our generation were brought up, into no one knows what."

Hansen's cautionary observations could just as well be applied today, which brings us to Japan and the sobering lessons it may offer us about our own future.

Takeaways

1. In an unfortunate turn for baby boomers, the US economy is struggling to recover from of one of the worst downturns in generations.

2. With fertility rates falling and longevity rising, the industrialized world is entering an unprecedented era of hyper-aging aggravated by population decline.

3. Adverse demographics are believed to be at the heart of what some prominent economists refer to as "secular stagnation," a long-term slowdown in economic activity, productivity and innovation that neither fiscal (tax) nor monetary (Fed) policies alone may be able to reverse.

4. In fact, tax increases and government benefit decreases may be forthcoming while life expectancy improve-ments result in a retirement that can last for 30 years or more.

5. Consequently, our personal nest eggs have taken on a level of importance they haven't previously had, and how you convert yours into a personal pension is critical to your long-term retirement success.

Questions for your financial advisor

1. Do you think our economy faces the risk of an extended period of secular stagnation and, if you do, how do you think my nest egg should be positioned to counteract any negative effects?

2. Is the possibility of a volatile economic future during my retirement years worthy of hedging against, and, if so, how?

3. Do you believe that our low rates of economic growth reflect bad tax policy predominantly and that corporate tax relief in the US will turn our economy around for the long term?

4. How reliable are my social security and pension benefits, and do you think I should start taking them or would it be better to defer them for as long as possible?

5. Can I retire before paying off all of my debt or should I keep working until I'm completely debt-free?

Chapter 2

THE HAUNTING

It would not be surprising if the 21ˢᵗ Century

turned out to be the Japanese Century.

Herman Kahn, Futurist
Time Magazine, 1970

I remember my surprise when I showed up to deliver a retirement seminar at a Connecticut country inn early one morning in the spring of 2009 to find a well-dressed Japanese couple sitting keen and alert in the very front row. While many people of Chinese, Korean and Indian descent had attended my presentations over the years, it was the first time for Japanese retirees. I secretly hoped they would request an appointment if only to share their experience as expats in the US and allow me to share my experience of living in Japan for a decade. They did, and at 10:00 am the following morning, Mr. Matsuda appeared—self-conscious, and without his wife. Aware of the custom of Japanese housewives controlling the purse strings, I confess to having been disappointed. I soon learned why they weren't together, though, as Mr. Matsuda unburdened himself, telling me a tale that has haunted me ever since.

A Cautionary Tale

Recently retired from a major Japanese trading giant with a large New York presence, Mr. Matsuda had been living with his wife of many years in a Connecticut suburb where they raised and educated their two grown children. He graduated from a top Tokyo university and had spent his entire career as a loyal sales executive for that one firm. His wife had dutifully followed him to the States over twenty years earlier, during Japan's booming mid-80s global expansion, to help further his career. But their relationship had grown rocky, not because of any unhappiness with America, but because of a poorly timed investment they made with her family inheritance.

After watching the Nikkei Industrial Index climb fourfold to nearly 40,000 between 1984 and 1989, Mr. Matsuda persuaded his wife that they had waited long enough for confirmation; it was time to invest in Japan's economic prowess and surging global dominance. They had already missed the run-up from 10,000 when they could have quadrupled their money and owed it to themselves and their family to get on board the 21st Century express. So, despite the unprecedented valuation levels reached by the market's index-leading stocks (price/earnings ratios well over 100x) and a sudden tightening of interest rates initiated by the Bank of Japan to protect the Yen, the Matsuda's decided in late 1989 to invest Mrs. Matsuda's $1 million inheritance—a disproportionate share of their nest egg—into Japan's world-beating stock market. To their chagrin, and like many retail investors, they got in at just the wrong time.

Less than a year later, the bubble had burst, and the market was down 50%. Shocked, but disciplined and anticipating a rebound, they decided to stay in stocks for the long run. A relief rally to 26,000 ensued but was short-lived. They were patient, enduring the market's ups and downs, and a rebound finally came when the market almost doubled from under 9,000 in 2003 to almost 18,000 in 2007, rekindling hope of a potential climb back to previous levels. Then came the global financial crisis. Between late 2007 and early 2009, the Nikkei average fell again by 56% to a new low of 7,428. Down 80% over 20 years, their $1 million nest egg was now worth $200,000: it would have to quintuple for them to (nominally) break even. Now older, Mr. Matsuda had recently retired on a pension nowhere near what he had been previously earning. Thinking about their long life expectancy and facing an extended retirement, the Matsuda's were beside themselves with anxiety. That's when they attended my seminar.

While they showed up at the inn together, it was only after Mrs. Matsuda had already read her husband the riot act. Because simply seeing his face reminded her of their financial calamity, she told him, Mrs. Matsuda declared Mr. Matsuda *persona non grata* in their home from 6:00 am to 6:00 pm every day. He was required to make himself scarce during the hours he would have previously been at work, so his new retirement lifestyle took the form of roaming the streets to stay out of his wife's line of sight. Like millions of other Japanese back home, he was learning to vanish, coping alone and under the radar with the shame, despair and grief that can accompany financial calamity and tear families apart. And that saga explained Mrs. Matsuda's absence.

At this writing, it's almost ten years later, the Matsuda's have since returned to Tokyo, and after nearly thirty years they watch as the Nikkei nears 22,000, just over halfway back to their entry point. Forty-five years old in 1989, they are now in their mid-70s, still waiting and hoping that their patrimony will be restored someday for their children, at least, if not to make their own retirements more comfortable. That remains to be seen. In the meantime, they have had to live with the effects of Japan's economic stagnation—including depressed asset values—for the bulk of their adult lives.

The Matsuda's experience has indelibly shaped my approach to retirement planning. I salute Mr. Matsuda for opening up about his predicament to me—a perfect stranger. Most of all, I am profoundly grateful to both of them for putting a human face on the lasting emotional trauma and interpersonal dislocation that can be inflicted by a shocking market crash followed by a decades-long drawdown. Grinding market losses like these can have wide ranging psychological as well as economic effects. Families—multiple generations—can be affected. Dreams crushed. Moods darkened. For me, their experience underscores that retirement portfolio planning has wide-ranging ramifications beyond mere percentage gains and losses and how important timing and loss avoidance are for ultimate success. Alas, good timing is often the result of sheer luck, while a proper respect for risk requires an accurate understanding of the mathematics of loss.

Japan as Economic Powerhouse

Currently owed roughly $1.1 trillion by the US, Japan has long been the leading single foreign buyer of US government debt. Despite its relatively small size, it remains the world's largest creditor nation, with over $3.3 trillion in net foreign assets accumulated during the glory days of the 1980s when its economy seemed unstoppable, its exports dominated world trade and the country seemed on track to surpass the US as the next global superpower. In 1970, when I first arrived there, Time Magazine ran an article titled "Toward the Japanese Century," which touted the nation's rapid growth and vast potential and introduced futurist Herman Kahn's prediction that "it would not be surprising if the 21st Century turned out to be the Japanese century." By 1979, Harvard sociologist Ezra Vogel had signaled Japan's arrival as an economic power in his international best seller "Japan as Number 1."

Japan had earned its status: In the 1970s Japan achieved the world's second largest gross national product (GNP) after the United States, and by the late 1980s ranked first in GNP per capita worldwide. In the 1980s, Japan's factories were humming, and its banks were the largest in the world in terms of market capitalization. Real estate and stock prices soared. Japan was buying up large chunks of the US and a one-square-mile plot under Tokyo's Imperial Palace was estimated to be worth all the real estate in California.

In his study of Japanese post-war economic development, Professor Shigeru Otsubo of Nagoya University explains that between 1955 and 1970, Japan had grown accustomed to strong economic growth of 9.5% per year. Between 1971 and 1990 growth averaged 3.8% annually. But after the collapse of its homegrown debt bubble in 1989, Japanese growth slowed, nominal GDP fell stagnant at less than 1% and the economy began operating far below capacity. Had Japan continued its 1980s growth trajectory it would have expanded its GDP from a 1989 peak of $5.7 trillion to almost $20 trillion today, rivaling if not exceeding the nominal 2016 US GDP of $18 trillion. Instead, Japan's GDP has stagnated over 27 years and remains what it was in 1990—enduring nearly three decades of foregone opportunity or, as expressed in economic shorthand, three "lost decades."

While economic growth stagnated, government spending to stimulate economic activity surged, outstripping tax revenues and increasing government debt. According to Japan's Ministry of Finance, government debt has climbed from a mere 20% of GDP in 1990 to over 250% today, the world's highest debt-to-GDP ratio (by a factor of 2x). Meanwhile in 2003 Japan's central bank implemented a zero interest rate policy (ZIRP), crushing the returns on savings and eventually forcing the closure of all Japanese money market funds, driving rates down in an effort to stimulate growth. The Bank of Japan (BOJ) has "printed" trillions of Yen to increase inflation to 2% from a negative 0.2% to no avail. Negative inflation has ensnared Japan in a deflationary price spiral. Deflation deters the already frugal Japanese from spending money today that could be worth more tomorrow. By 2015 ten-year Japanese Government Bonds (JGBs) were being issued at negative rates of interest, requiring lenders to pay for the privilege of parting with their money!

But nothing helped. To date, none of these moves were able to turn the economic tide of an aging population and shrinking workforce. The fact is that Japan's "core" population ages 0-64 peaked in 1989—the year the bubble burst—and has been declining since. As described by demographer Chris Hamilton, "between 1965 and 1989, Japan's core population rose 16 million. Since 1989, it has decreased by 17 million. While Japan's core population was growing, its GDP grew rapidly without increasing government debt. Since Japan's population began shrinking, GDP growth has slowed to a crawl and, according to Finance Ministry data, Japanese debt to GDP has soared from 67% to more than 250%."

In 1989, Mitsubishi Estate Company bought a 51 percent stake in New York City's Rockefeller Center, symbolizing for many Japan's emerging global economic dominance. A foreign visitor to the tourist district of any of its major cities even today would reasonably conclude that everything was still fine and that Japanese culture—non-violent, polite, collaborative and creative—offered many admirable features for global emulation. So, on many measures Japan remains a very rich nation of educated, famously hard-working people enjoying lifelong employment at paternalistic corporations, ready to do whatever it takes to achieve success. For those middle-aged and older who entered the system in the good years from the 1960s to the 1980s, retirement can be comfortable; after all, they are believed to hold 80% of Japan's financial wealth. But we can no longer count on the Japanese to be a major buyer of US government debt because Japan has become a net seller—to help finance its own generous social security benefits, amounting to over 30% of government spending that is owed to a growing number of citizens 65 and over, who also happen to enjoy the most extended longevity in the world today.

Japan as Canary in the Coal Mine

If the 21st Century will indeed be remembered as the Japanese century, it may be because Japan was the first to confront the industrialized world's deteriorating demographic trends, experiment with debt-based solutions, and then model the consequences in the form of "lost decades" of economic stagnation. What were the associated costs? Reduced expectations and social malaise borne predominantly by gloomy millennials notoriously uninterested in procreation and family formation. I highly doubt this is what Herman Kahn had in mind.

The reality is that Japan's economic and social profile is being shaped by its pace-setting adverse demographics. Because of a current fertility rate under 1.5 and a shrinking population of women in their 20s and 30s, Japan's population is forecast to decline from its current level of 128 million to around 90 million by 2050, and 47 million by 2100. (Some have observed that based on the present rate of decline, in 600 years there will be only 480 Japanese left). The UN's Center for Strategic and International Studies has predicted that by 2030 the elderly (age 65 and older) will comprise over 30% of Japan's total population on their way to 40% in 2050, at which point Japan will have a median age of 52, making it the oldest society ever known. For every two retirees, there will be around three working people, down from six in 1990, for a support ratio of approximately 1.5 to 1.

As of this writing, current sales of adult diapers in Japan exceed those intended for babies. From a high of 2.7 million in 1949, the Japan Times reports that births hit a record low of 981,000 in 2016, and for the first year in over 100 there were fewer births recorded than deaths. In preparing for the future, Japanese ingenuity is heavily focused on the role of robotics. Japan *needs* robots. Among millennials, male and female relationships with digital avatars are said to be increasingly popular, often deemed less complicated (and far less expensive) than those with real people.

Thus, rather than a vision of growing wealth and promise, "Japanification" has become a dark foreshadowing of the future for all advanced countries concerned that they will follow Japan's example, rendering lost decades of economic opportunity the norm. The age wave has stopped the Japanese economic juggernaut in its tracks, and to date no amount of financial engineering has been able to change that reality. Nor has it helped the Japanese stock market regain its previous highs, which offers US retirees—especially the readers of this book—a sobering lesson.

The Nikkei Crash of '89

Japan's bellwether Nikkei Industrial Index is a price-weighted stock market index for the Tokyo Stock Exchange. The Nikkei Crash of 1989 ranks as one of the three greatest stock market crashes of all time (the other two being American) and its effects are still being felt.

FIGURE 5. JAPAN'S NIKKEI STOCK INDEX COLLIDED WITH THE AGE WAVE TRIGGERING "LOST DECADES" OF SECULAR STAGNATION

In December 1989, the "Nikkei 225" peaked at 38,916 closing out a triumphant decade. It began the 1980s below 7,000, pushed above 10,000 by August 1984, and went on from there to nearly quadruple in just five years, routinely outperforming the rest of the world's stock markets. Its surge coincided with the printing of new Yen by the BOJ to encourage domestic consumption and investment. The sudden and dramatic increase in domestic money supply led to speculation: stock and real estate prices climbed. In 1989, worried about soaring home prices, the BOJ suddenly reversed course by lifting interest rates from 2.5% to 6.0%, putting a brake on the mania that had been fueled by its earlier easy-money regime. The Nikkei started a descent. As tracked by MacroTrends, it dropped in stages, losing 37% in 1990, followed by a more bearable 5% in 1991, and then 23% more in 1992, for a total collapse of 56% over three years. Ten years later, in 2003 it finally bottomed at 7,608 for a peak-to-trough collapse of 80%. It revisited that low again in 2009, then drifted sideways for four years through 2013, before rising at this writing five years later to just above 22,800. In other words, after 27 years, it's still over 40% below its 1989 high!

No retiree invested in equities would ever want to be caught in this type of market. First, the crash occurred in stages, enticing the well-trained and trusting investor to hold on despite initial losses, choosing to believe that losses were temporary and positioning the index for a rebound. Since the greater the loss the greater the potential snapback, the logic goes, it might even be tempting to "buy the dip" and some investors may have committed even more capital.

Second, at full extension, the decline was crushing, amounting to an 80% loss. Third, the exhausting climb to just over halfway back after 27 years—longer than the duration of today's average retirement—has required that holdings be sold at prices lower than originally paid if needed to provide income. A forced sale into a down market triggering losses has to be every investor's nightmare, while a seemingly endless recovery has to be every retiree's financial calamity. Few retirement plans could survive a crash of this magnitude and duration without imposing serious belt-tightening and lifestyle compromise.

Our Crash of '29

Could it happen here? It can, and it already has. As measured by the Dow Jones Industrial Average (DJIA), the Nikkei's experience is eerily comparable to the greatest collapse in American history, the traumatic stock market crash of 1929 that preceded the Great Depression. The DJIA is a price-weighted average of 30 actively traded "blue chip" stocks, primarily industrials but also including financials and other service-oriented companies. The components, which change from time to time, represent between 15% and 20% of the market value of all the stocks listed on the New York Stock Exchange (NYSE).

The Great Crash of '29 too followed an asset bubble: starting in 1921, the stock market had surged nearly 20% per year to quadruple in value by its 1929 peak. A growing swath of the public invested thanks to the financial invention of buying on margin, which allowed people to borrow money from their banks and brokers with only 10-20 percent down, using the securities purchased to serve as collateral, which contributed to the irrational exuberance of the Roaring Twenties.

FIGURE 6. THE GREAT (AMERICAN) CRASH OF '29

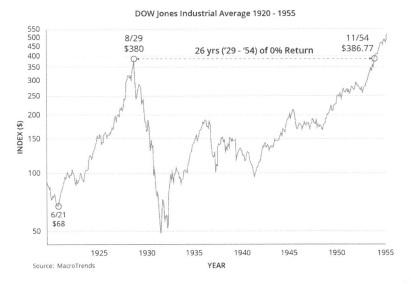

DOW Jones Industrial Average 1920 - 1955

Source: MacroTrends

Over the course of the 1920s boom, the Dow climbed from a low of 68 in 1921 to a high of 380 in late August 1929, a rise of almost 440% over the decade. From there it fell 20% in a "mere" bear market correction to around 300 in late October. On Black Monday – October 28th, 1929 – the Dow fell 13% to 260 followed by Black Tuesday, which saw a drop of 12% to 230. From the high in late August through late November '29, a period of about 70 days, the market had dropped 47%: investors were triggered and sold in a panic. Sure enough, over the next five months the DJIA rose by 48% to 300, and it was only from April into late December 1930 that it crashed another 47% to 150, and from there to its bottom of 40 in July 1932, for a peak-to-trough loss of 90% over three years. Once the bottom was finally reached, the market gradually rose, but it wasn't until November 1954 that it got back to its 1929 peak. It took over 26 years to recover.

The 1929 Wall Street crash and 1989 Nikkei collapse share many remarkable similarities. But there is at least one major difference between the two events: twenty years after the 1932 bottom the Depression had ended, and the Dow was in a clear uptrend. Twenty years on in Japan, and the Nikkei was still sinking to new lows. While it has since recovered to 22,800 with help from BOJ stock purchasing, that still leaves (at this writing) another 75% gain needed before the Nikkei recovers its 1989 high. In other words, it has taken 27 years for the Nikkei to climb just over half way back! Will it take another decade or two before it returns to its former peak?

And what might explain this key difference in duration between these two seminal market events? It's certainly worth noting that in 1950 the American baby boom was getting underway and would ultimately provide the impetus for decades of economic growth; in contrast, Japan hit the age-wave wall in 1989, leading to decades of economic stagnation. Does this suggest that the next Wall Street crash, under aging demographic conditions paralleling the Japanese model, could require a much longer recovery period? It's certainly possible.

This is the worst-case scenario that should haunt every retiree and financial advisor when constructing a retirement portfolio: The assumption that equities will outperform all other asset classes over the long run has to be tempered by the realization that the long run, as in Japan, can be too long. Most retirees simply cannot afford to get ensnared in a bottoming stock or bond market for what could turn out to be almost the entire duration of their retirement! Avoiding this downside risk in retirement portfolios is, in my opinion, job number one.

We May Be Wrong

We must always be mindful that we can be off in our expectations and predictions and that our fears of adverse outcomes may be overblown. After all, the US is not Japan and maybe we're making too much of demographic drag. Perhaps lighter regulatory policies and business tax relief (with or without more central bank money "printing") can generate the needed economic stimulus and employment growth. Maybe asset prices have no place to go but up simply because the powers that be want it that way. In that case, you would certainly not want your retirement portfolio to miss out on the opportunity to participate and capture at least a share of any upside potential ahead.

The FIA enables retirees to hedge this dilemma. It's an insurance contract engineered to help protect you from sudden market declines and interminable market recoveries while positioning you to participate when markets rise. It might even enable you to grow your nest egg over a multi-year Nikkei-like scenario. That's why I believe it may be well-suited to serve as the anchor of a "stable-core" retirement portfolio.

If you can, you'll want to confer with your financial advisor and make defensive moves *before* a market decline. When they occur, corrections and crashes tend to surprise in terms of timing, magnitude and duration. Most of us can little afford to let our retirement nest eggs get caught up in one. Using the FIA, you can take positive steps to help manage downside risk without having to move to the sidelines by going to cash or bonds and abandoning further equity market advances. As always, timing is key.

Takeaways

1. Indices are unmanaged, and investors cannot invest directly in them. Unless otherwise noted, performance of indices does not account for any fees, commissions or other expenses that would be incurred. Returns do not include reinvested dividends.

2. The Japanese economy was stopped in its tracks by the age wave and to date no amount of financial engineering has been able to revive it.

3. As a consequence, the Japanese people have suffered almost three decades of lost economic opportunity—foreshadowing the secular stagnation that may overhang all industrial nations today, including our own.

4. Starting in late 1989 Japan's Nikkei 225 Industrial Index crashed 80% and, at this writing 28 years later, has recovered just over half its peak value, even after repeated BOJ interventions.

5. A lengthy market downturn can happen here too, and has: It took the Dow Jones Industrial Average over 26 years to recover after the crash of '29, undermining many investors who retired relying on stocks.

Questions for your financial advisor

1. Do you think our stock market's upward trajectory is limitless, or would it be prudent to hedge against an inevitable reversal?

2. What do you make of the Nikkei's drawn-out downturn, and is there any evidence such a thing could happen here?

3. Do you think Japan's "lost decades" tell us anything about our own economic prospects?

4. Why did it take 25 years for the Dow Jones Industrial Index to recover after the 90% crash of '29-'32, and do you think there's any chance we might get hit with another Great Crash and prolonged recovery?

5. What happens to my retirement income projections if my portfolio tracks the S&P 500 Stock Index and the index drops 50% as it did from 2000-2002 and 2007-2009, but takes a decade or two to recover?

Chapter 3

TIME IS MONEY

Teach us to count our days
that we may envision the future
with a wizened heart.

Psalms 90:12

When urging clients in their mid-to-late 80s to get proactive about their "long-term" financial planning, I often relate the remarkable story of Dr. Ingeborg Rapoport. It brings home not only the indomitable power of the human spirit, but also the truly amazing advances in human life expectancy that have been achieved over the last century—and continue to be made with increasing velocity.

Dr. Rapoport had already been retired for thirty years when Hamburg University authorities finally gave her a chance to complete her doctoral degree—but only after following all the rules. She would have to stand for an oral exam, questioned face to face by a panel of academics, to defend her original dissertation on diphtheria. The dissertation had been well received when she first submitted it at the tender age of 25, but she was blocked by the Nazi regime from completing the process because her mother was Jewish. Although she went on to enjoy a professional career in neonatal medicine she always felt unfairly deprived and, after 77 years, wanted to right what she felt was an injustice. Now nearly blind, it was only with the help of friends that she was able to catch up on developments in diphtheria studies during the intervening decades.

Dr. Rapoport passed her exams with no age-based indulgences and was finally awarded her degree in 2015, becoming the oldest person ever to be awarded a doctorate, according to Guinness World Records.

She was 102.

And that's the point: Underlying successful retirement planning at any age today is an appreciation of contemporary developments in longevity. No matter your starting point, if you're in reasonably good health you're advised to play the long game.

Perceiving Time

Retirement clock management begins with the very first questions posed in the planning process: "*When* can I (afford to) retire? Can it be *sooner*, does it have to wait until *later* or will it be *never*? And by the way, *how long* should I expect my retirement to last?"

Answering these fundamental questions starts with an appreciation of the defining risk in 21st Century retirement—living to age 100, or beyond. True, not all of us will make it that long. But when a husband and wife aged 65 visit with me, and they're in reasonably good health, I have to inform them that, statistically, one member of the pair, usually the female, has a 50% chance of making it to age 94 and a 25% chance of making it all the way to age 98—which really isn't that far from 100, is it? And if she makes it to 98, she has a 50% chance of making it all the way to triple digits, because actuarial science informs us that the longer we live, the better our odds of further survival.

FIGURE 7. MOST RETIREES ARE NAIVELY COMPLACENT ABOUT LONGEVITY RISK

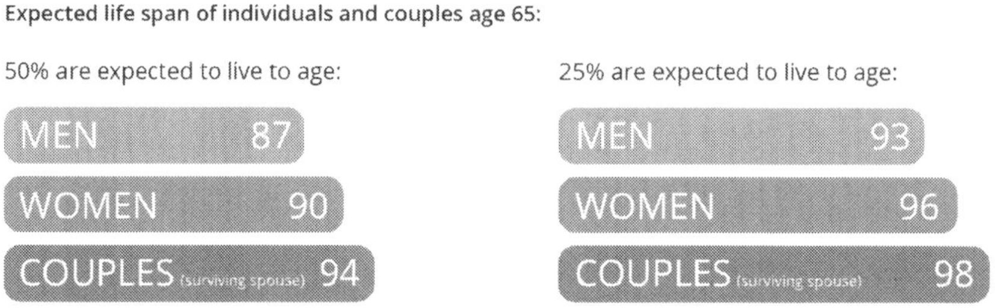

Expected life span of individuals and couples age 65:

50% are expected to live to age:

MEN   87
WOMEN   90
COUPLES (surviving spouse)   94

25% are expected to live to age:

MEN   93
WOMEN   96
COUPLES (surviving spouse)   98

Source: Society of Actuaries

The wealthier and better educated the individual, the more life expectancy improves. If, as frequently happens, one spouse turns out to be ten years younger when the primary earner reaches full retirement, then to be prudent we should be planning for a forty-five-year joint cash flow. Fundamentally, my task as a retirement planner comes down to helping clients make sure the cash flow the longer-lived survivor may need thirty, forty or even fifty years from now will show up on schedule—ideally adjusted for inflation to preserve its purchasing power. Portfolio design follows on from that core purpose. Thus, our first objective is to figure out how to guarantee a lifelong cash flow under extended and extenuating circumstances.

A recent World Economic Forum white paper on increasing longevity shows how steadily life expectancy has increased since the mid-20th Century and continues to increase. According to the white paper, a child born in 2007 has a median life expectancy of 104 in the US and 107 in Japan. That means that, at this writing, half the ten-year-olds alive in both countries will live longer than 104 or 107! How much longer? Maybe a lot if health technologies continue to advance. So the paper's operative question, "how can we afford it?" is answered "we can't." That is, not unless we make some wide-ranging changes in our attitude toward retirement (people will need to work far longer) and in our outdated retirement financing systems designed to support durations of 15, 20 or at the outside, 30 years.

So, it turns out that longevity—what I term "back-end" retirement risk—isn't simply extended, it's open-ended. If so, managing assets to provide for endless cash flows is like trying to score a touchdown when the goalposts keep receding. Retirement's "open-ended back end" distinguishes spend-down planning from all other forms of target-dated "accumulation" strategies. If you're 45 years old and know that you expect to retire at 65, you've got 20 years to accumulate a nest egg at the "front end" and there are guidelines you can follow to get it done. But once you retire at 65, you have no idea how many years that nest egg will need to last—nor would your advisor—so the rules and methods that worked during the "ac-cumulation" phase may not work at all during the "de-cumulation" phase.

Essentially, retirement planning aims to manage some very unique variables in the interplay of time and money. Its operational goal is the generation of lifelong cash flows from sources other than human capital—i.e., your paid labor—to replace previously earned income in amounts sufficient to match your expenses. To truly succeed, it must protect, and if possible, enhance the value of your purchasing power over an open-ended time horizon. To do so, the process pits two antagonistic forces against each other: one, the force of compound interest that increases wealth over time; the other, the force of monetary inflation that erodes wealth over time.

These two forces have opposite economic and financial effects: In an inflationary environment, time reduces money's worth and therefore accelerates its use. In a deflationary environment, time enhances money's worth and defers its use to another day when it will buy more. The longer the time horizon in which these forces play out, the more pronounced the antagonistic outcomes. Thirty years of inflation at 3% results in a 60% loss of buying power; three decades of compounding 3% interest can produce a 140% increase in buying power. That's a 200% spread, making this a battle that is absolutely worth fighting.

Your Time Horizon

Ironically, unless you made it a practice to think decades ahead when you were younger, it's now – as you enter the final phase of your life's journey – that you must seriously begin doing so. To effectively deal with the financial effects of unprecedented longevity—to play the long game—you need to cultivate a very long view. And let's face it: unlike the Japanese and Chinese, thinking long term is not something we Americans are known for.

The mainstream media are of little help, inundating us with sales messages that fail to put us in the right frame of mind. In my office, for example, we are surrounded by flat-panel TVs tuned to the financial cable networks reporting from open to close—premarket to aftermarket—every major market tick. Pundits mostly young enough to have never been burned by a bear market report breathlessly about individual stocks and indices moving up or down here or abroad, as if tracking their hour-to-hour price performance was the only appropriate focus for an investor's financial attention.

This may be true for a day-trader. But investment time horizons range dramatically depending on methodology and objectives. For the technology-driven high frequency trader it's measured in milliseconds. The equity analyst and corporate CEO share a three-month horizon focused on profit performance. Most portfolio managers selling separate account or mutual fund results report over 1, 3, 5 and 10-year periods.

The retirement investor needs an even longer time horizon. I recommend a total of sixty years, twenty over the front-end if you get started early enough and forty to cover the back-end if you should live so long. Sixty years is the length of a Kondratieff Wave, for goodness sake. According to Kondratieff—the eminent Russian economist executed by Stalin in 1938 because his cyclical theory of economic history (which started back in 10th Century China) applauded the emergence of free markets—nations and their economies pass through four full life-cycle seasons during recurring sixty-year periods, undergoing every possible financial and economic permutation. If true, a long-term retirement portfolio must be designed to respond effectively to each of those seasons—spring, summer, fall, and winter, and it must unfold and perform over a sixty-year-plus time horizon.

FIGURE 8. FOUR K WAVES IN THE UNITED STATES

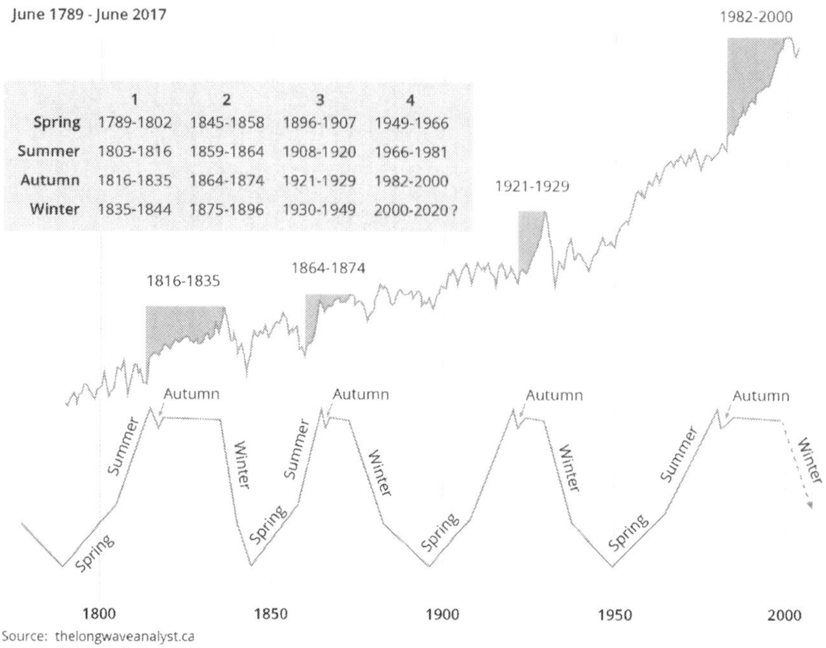

June 1789 - June 2017

1982-2000

	1	2	3	4
Spring	1789-1802	1845-1858	1896-1907	1949-1966
Summer	1803-1816	1859-1864	1908-1920	1966-1981
Autumn	1816-1835	1864-1874	1921-1929	1982-2000
Winter	1835-1844	1875-1896	1930-1949	2000-2020?

1921-1929

1864-1874

1816-1835

Autumn

Summer

Spring

Winter

Autumn

Summer

Spring

Winter

Autumn

Spring

Winter

Autumn

Summer

Spring

Winter

1800   1850   1900   1950   2000

Source: thelongwaveanalyst.ca

While taking a long-term approach, performance sensitivity to much shorter durations also has to be properly tuned. Seeking safety and simplicity, two retiring lighting designers, husband and wife, brought me their IRAs back in 2005. Invested in FIAs, both portfolios were linked to the same index, the S&P 500 Composite, and gains were set to be captured by means of the same methodology. The two portfolios were identical except for one feature: their market participation started two days apart. Results achieved for the year ending in 2017 are illustrative: over twelve months, the first IRA earned 7.18%, the second 4.08%, a full 43% less. The only difference between them? Two specific calendar days of market exposure!

FIGURE 9. YOUR RETIREMENT OUTCOME IS LARGELY A MATTER OF TIMING

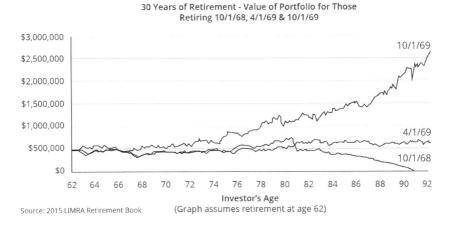

30 Years of Retirement - Value of Portfolio for Those
Retiring 10/1/68, 4/1/69 & 10/1/69

Source: 2015 LIMRA Retirement Book (Graph assumes retirement at age 62)

The starting date's impact on a 30-year retirement can be startling. Figure 9 shows the outcomes after thirty years for a standard "investment policy" portfolio consisting of 60% stocks and 40% bonds after withdrawals of 4.05% increased every year (by 3%) to keep up with inflation. The start dates range over a 12-month period from October 1968 to October 1969. Had you retired in April 1969, after 30 years your portfolio would have been worth pretty much the same as where it started; had you retired 6 months later, after thirty years you would have accumulated five times more than what you started with! Alas, if you kicked off your retirement in October 1968, after thirty years you'd be broke. That's a wide breadth of long-term outcomes initiated over a rather narrow twelve-month range of start dates, don't you think? The outcomes are attributable solely to the unpredictable and random effects of timing, or what we refer to in the vernacular as "luck."

The wide variation in outcomes is the result of real-world unpredictability. We don't know what returns will actually be realized by the asset classes in our portfolios over the specific time frames we'll be holding them, so we often base our planning—and expectations—on historical averages. But when it comes to retirement planning, average returns can be misleading. It's the sequence of actual year-by-year returns that is much more informative. For retirees, the order of returns takes pre-eminence over their magnitude.

FIGURE 10. RETURN SEQUENCE MAKES ALL THE DIFFERENCE

S&P 500 Index Sequence of Returns

Year	Clockwise 1989-2008	Counter-Clockwise 2008-1989
1	31.69	-37.00
2	-3.11	5.49
3	30.47	15.84
4	7.62	4.91
5	10.08	10.88
6	1.32	28.68
7	37.58	-22.10
8	22.96	-11.88
9	33.36	-9.11
10	28.58	21.04
11	21.04	28.58
12	-9.11	33.36
13	-11.88	22.96
14	-22.10	37.58
15	28.68	1.32
16	10.88	10.08
17	4.91	7.62
18	15.84	30.47
19	5.49	-3.11
20	-37.00	31.69
Average Annual Total Return:	8.43%	8.43%

Past performance does not guarantee future results.
Source: Standard & Poor's, Annual Returns for the period 1989-2008
Courtesy: Thornburg Investment Management

Thornburg
INVESTMENT MANAGEMENT

This vital factor is illustrated in Figure 10, which sets forth the S&P 500 total returns generated over the 20-year period from 1989-2008. The average return over the period was 8.43%. The first thing to notice is that no single year actually produced a return equal to the average; returns ranged from losses as great as -37% to gains as high as +38%. The second is to note that if we reverse the sequence we end up with the same average annual return. So, if we start with $1 million and take no withdrawals, then after twenty years we end up with the same total accumulation ($5,044,343) no matter whether the losses came first or the gains came first.

Of course, the experience of getting to the end result couldn't have been more different. The clockwise (historical) sequence produced rather comfortable gains (32%) right out of the gate and fairly consistently over the first ten years, maybe enough to engender some self-satisfied investor complacency. By contrast, the counterclockwise (reversed) sequence starts out with a painful loss (-37%) that the portfolio would need to scramble to recover during its first ten years, very likely generating at least a modicum of investor stress and even self-doubt. Fortunately, the reverse sequence provided a hefty bounce (32%) in the final year that brought its portfolio up to the level of the historical portfolio; yes, markets can surely amaze. The historical portfolio, however, suffered the bad luck of a rather painful loss (-37%) during that final accumulation year immediately ahead of theoretical retirement, demonstrating just how cruel markets can be sometimes.

FIGURE 11. EFFECT OF RETURN SEQUENCE ON PORTFOLIOS UNDERGOING SYSTEMATIC WITHDRAWALS

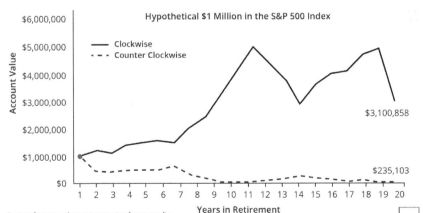

Past performance does not guarantee future results.
Source: Standard & Poor's and Bureau of Labor Statistics; calculated by Thornburg Investment Management
$50,000 was withdrawn in year one; withdrawal amount was increased by the change in the Consumer Price Index
(CPI-U) each year (3.05% average for the period)

If we add a 5% annual withdrawal from each hypothetical portfolio (increased each year by the change in the Consumer Price Index (CPI-U)) we quickly see the lift that early positive returns can provide as opposed to the squeamish belt-tightening that can be imposed by early losses. In the income phase of retirement, return sequence makes all the difference, especially in terms of what's left and the emotional stress we may endure during the process. The clockwise sequence left a theoretical retiree with a $3.1 million asset pool at the end of twenty years available for spend-down over the next twenty; the counter-clockwise sequence would have left the same retiree with a miniscule $235,000 that would have to be stretched over a decade or two!

It's to the sequence of actual returns that we respond as both investors and human beings. The retiree who lost 37% during the final accumulation year wouldn't be happy about losing $3 million after choosing to stay invested those last twelve months while perched on the retirement threshold; the retiree who gained $1.2 million over that same final accumulation year may feel appropriately rewarded for acumen and market discipline. This disparity in outcomes infuses the debate between advocates of a buy-and-hold approach and the more tactical approach that advocates a buy-hold-sell discipline. As illustrated in Figure 12, courtesy of Economist Lance Roberts, over the 20 years since 1998, a portfolio tracking the S&P 500 index that missed the 10 worst days in the market would have significantly outperformed an otherwise identical portfolio that missed the ten best. It's a powerful demonstration of the fact that first, over the long run, tactical asset management can sometimes outperform a more passive buy-and-hold approach and that, second, loss-avoidance can be more valuable than return maximization.

FIGURE 12. AVOIDING LOSSES CAN BE MORE VALUABLE THAN MISSING GAINS

—— $100,000 Missing 10 Best Days   ---- $100,000 Missing 10 Worst Days   ····· $100,000 Invested in Index (Buy & Hold)

Courtesy: Lance Roberts, RealInvestmentAdvice.com

So, is time spent passively invested "in" the market recommended for long-term results, or is a more active approach that tries to identify sell signals and entry points to "time" the market a truly more effective alternative? Unfortunately, extreme market action tends to be random and unpredictable. Some market signals may work some of the time, but I've never found a system to time market shifts that works every time (other than in retrospect). Have you?

Figure 12 shows rather conclusively that at least since 1998 avoiding bad losses contributed more to portfolio growth than capturing maximum gains. That's because losses take precious time to recover. Since 1945, the average of the 12 bear markets we've experienced has lasted 14 months and triggered a loss of just over 30%. The math of loss tells us that to recover from a 30% loss requires a 43% gain; moreover, a retirement portfolio in the commonly recommended 4% withdrawal mode will require a three-year recovery of 63%. Returns of this magnitude are exceedingly rare. In other words, corrections and bear markets have tangible consequences in retirement; they can trigger anxiety and necessitate belt-tightening to buy the time needed for a nest egg to recover.

The Eighth Wonder

Of course, time spent recovering would be much better spent compounding new wealth. But wait: markets don't compound. They earn "returns"—both positive and negative. Depending on the sequence of those returns, wealth may grow or shrink. Compounding on the other hand is a unidirectional growth process: it consists of the earning of interest on interest-previously-earned-and-reinvested. To work its magic, compounding requires a constant capital sum and consistency—*over as much time as possible.* The more time allotted to the process, the more powerful the effect. Legend has it that Einstein declared the process of compounding to be the eighth wonder of the world and the most powerful force in nature. Time is part and parcel of compounding; it is its necessary substratum. The longer the process has to work, the greater the predictable end result.

FIGURE 13. COMPOUNDING GROWS WEALTH

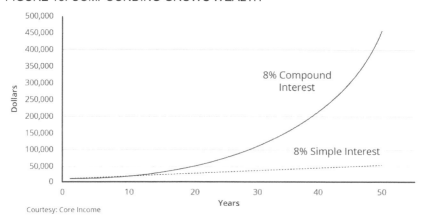

Courtesy: Core Income

In the obverse, time can have an outright negative impact on market returns. Decades of growth can be permanently lost. Consider a recent decade of lost returns. If you had invested in the S&P 500 Composite Index on January 1, 2000, your investment at the end of 2009 would have been down 24%. Your average annual return for that ten-year period: -2.14%. Or think about it this way: if you had been invested in March 1929 tracking the DJIA from its peak at 350 and stayed invested, it would have taken to November 1954 to recover the value lost. Your average annual return over that twenty-six-year period: 0%. Had you compounded your money at 3% over that same period, you would have doubled it.

FIGURE 14. MARKETS DON'T COMPOUND; THEY GENERATE "RETURNS," BOTH POSITIVE AND NEGATIVE

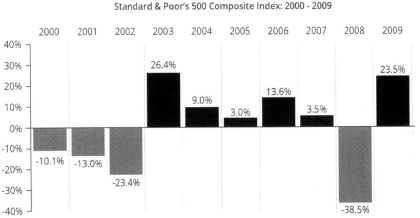

Standard & Poor's 500 Composite Index: 2000 - 2009

Source: MSNMoney.com. Market returns represented by S&P 500 Price Return Index. Returns assume no reinvestment of dividends and reflect calendar year returns, not peak to trough. Past performance is not indicative of future returns.

Time exerts another critical influence on returns because it renders markets cyclical. Markets breathe. They rise and fall over time. They never move in any one direction forever. The passage of time increases the likelihood of a change in trend. The longer and more pronounced a trend, the sooner it can be expected to reach an inflection point that reverses its direction to complete its cycle. The longer and lower markets fall, the more likely they will be to reach a bottom and reverse course. What are those critical inflection points and when will they be reached? Many market technicians and historians have developed complex theories and abstruse formulae designed to pinpoint tops and bottoms to forecast optimal market exit and entry points. Over the three decades I've spent as a student of this process, I've arrived at one conclusion: markets are unpredictable.

FIGURE 15. MARKETS ARE CYCLICAL; THE GOOD TIMES NEVER LAST FOREVER

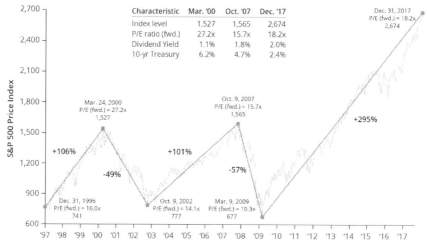

Characteristic	Mar. '00	Oct. '07	Dec. '17
Index level	1,527	1,565	2,674
P/E ratio (fwd.)	27.2x	15.7x	18.2x
Dividend Yield	1.1%	1.8%	2.0%
10-yr Treasury	6.2%	4.7%	2.4%

Source: Compustat, Factset, Thomson Reuters, Federal Reserve, Standard & Poor's J.P. Morgan Asset Management. Dividend yield is calculated as consensus estimates of dividends for the next 12 months, divided by consensus estimates for earnings in the next 12 months (NTM), and is provided by FactSet Market Aggregates. Returns are cumulative and based on S&P 500 Index price movement only, and do not include the reinvestment of dividends. Past performance is not indicative of future returns. *Guide to the Markets - U.S.* Data are as of December 31, 2017.

J.P.Morgan
Asset Management

Whether bull or bear, financial markets reflect the cyclical nature of their underlying economies. The business cycle affects security pricing via the fundamentals of revenues and profits that are reflected in valuation. Meanwhile, economies as a whole go through sequential periods of expansion and contraction, inflation and deflation, boom and bust. The societies that shape those economies have their own demographic, sociological, political and ideological characteristics that evolve and change over time. And then there are the global linkages that drive geopolitical developments out of the control of any one country or alliance of nations.

FIGURE 16. WE CAN BE AFFECTED BY CYCLES OF WHICH WE CAN BE TOTALLY UNAWARE

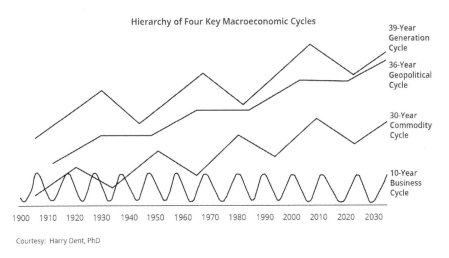

Hierarchy of Four Key Macroeconomic Cycles

39-Year Generation Cycle

36-Year Geopolitical Cycle

30-Year Commodity Cycle

10-Year Business Cycle

1900 1910 1920 1930 1940 1950 1960 1970 1980 1990 2000 2010 2020 2030

Courtesy: Harry Dent, PhD

There is an entire school of economists today that believes the American economy may be approaching a negative inflection point, for a variety of reasons—demographic imbalance, over-indebtedness, income and wealth inequality, corporate cronyism, political corruption, hubris, greed, war—you name it. Whether it's based on the 60-year Kondratieff Wave, the generational Elliott Wave, the 120-year Kress cycle or William Stanley Jevons' declining sun spot activity cycle, there is a convergence of big-picture cycle analysis that suggests the US economy could be approaching, entering or already in a major downturn.

An extended economic downturn reflected in declining markets could not come at a worse time for baby boomers launching the retirement phase of their own lifecycle. I've followed these market theorists for many years. In the short term their timing has been off and plenty of their predictions have been wrong, although sometimes they've been uncannily accurate. We can hope that they're wrong, but it would be imprudent to completely ignore their warnings.

What if an economic storm *is* bearing down on us? Given that inflection points are reached when least expected, hit us hard and leave us dazed, how should retirees be battening down the hatches? It is we, after all, who must prepare for the worst, protecting our hard-earned wealth from a sudden, adverse change in market direction.

On the other hand, what if the sky doesn't fall (so soon)? What if our worst fears are misplaced and markets continue to rise (before inevitably falling, as they must, to complete a full market cycle)? We surely want to participate as long as we can and while conditions permit.

With all its limitations, the FIA at the heart of the stable core portfolio is designed to make timing the market unnecessary, by providing downside protection at inflection points together with upside participation before, during and after a correction or crash. It enables you to behave like a fearless market champion by taming your flight instinct while exposing you to upside potential at all times. It helps protects you from yourself, insulating you from some of your most self-destructive investor behavior—namely buying and selling at all the wrong times.

Driven by greed and fear, average investor behavior usually results in sub-par performance. But you can't help it and I don't have the skills to serve as your market-behavior therapist. Rather, my job is to help you understand the value of having a solid core in your retirement portfolio to help protect it—and you—from impulses to buy and sell at inopportune moments.

That I *can* do.

Takeaways

1. Retirement planning starts with assuring that your nest egg (with or without inputs from other income sources) serves as a personal pension guaranteeing you the paychecks you'll need for 30-40 years after you stop working.

2. As an investor, you need to understand that time is of the essence and that playing the long game means hedging against numerous long-term cyclical risks decades in advance of their possible impact.

3. Once you begin to spend down, retirement success depends more upon the sequence of returns you earn than the annual magnitude of those returns.

4. To make your nest egg last for the long run, best practice is to focus on avoiding sharp losses rather than seeking high returns.

5. True compounding will yield a more predictable outcome than the generation of random market returns that can offset each other, reduce the net result to zero (or less) and waste your precious time.

Questions for your financial advisor

1. Just how long does my (our) nest egg have to last me (us) in retirement?

2. Will I run out of money if I outlive my life expectancy, and if I do, whom do you suggest I call?

3. My wife's mother is 98 years old and going strong: can you show me (us) how to plan for an open-ended lifespan—just in case one of us lives much longer than expected?

4. How would your income and wealth accumulation projections be impacted by a lost decade of negative returns at the outset of my (our) retirement?

5. What would I (we) have to do to respond constructively to a lost decade of negative returns during the second decade of my (our) retirement?

Chapter 4

MINDING YOUR BEHAVIOR

The emotions of investing have destroyed far more
potential investment return than the economics of investing
have ever dreamed of destroying.

John Bogle
Founder, Vanguard Group

My first stock market crash began at the opening bell. Recently minted, I was a "financial advisor" for just over a year when Black Monday unfolded. What a day October 19, 1987 proved to be. Starting in Hong Kong and blowing through Europe, a chain reaction of market distress sent world stock exchanges plummeting in a matter of hours. As described by Donald Bernhardt and Marshall Eckblad in their report to the Federal Reserve Bank of Chicago, there was no sanctuary. In the United States, the DJIA dropped 22.6% in one day's trading, a loss that remains the largest single-session stock market decline in history and the sharpest market downturn since the

Great Depression. If Black Monday were to happen at today's price levels, it would be a single day's loss in the Dow of over 5,000 points! Think about that. Over three consecutive trading days back then, the S&P 500 lost a combined 28.5% of its value. No exaggeration there. Twenty-eight and a half percent was lost in just over 24 hours of trading.

I took calls that day from panicked investors who were in the process of moving their pension assets to my supervision. Unable to get through to their brokers with sell orders, they were seeking my assurance that all would not be lost forever. Of course, even if their brokers had taken their calls, the sheer number of sell orders that day vastly outnumbered buy offers anywhere near previous prices. That lack of liquidity—i.e., the absence of buyers—in the face of panic selling is what gave rise to the downward cascade in stock markets in the first place.

This crash was different because it was truly a global event. For the first time, it brought home to American investors—including many baby boomers entering their prime earning years and just starting to invest—the interconnected nature of markets around the world. Donald Marron, chairman of Paine Webber, a prominent investment firm at the time, underscored the new reality: "Nowhere is that (inter-relatedness) exemplified more than people staying up all night to watch the Japanese market to get a feeling for what might happen in the next session of the New York market."

You had to have been there to get a sense of the fear that overtook otherwise rational investors and hardened financial professionals alike. As reported by the Chicago Fed, stock markets everywhere had raced upward during the first half of 1987. By late August, the DJIA had gained 44% in a matter of seven months, leading some observers to worry that the market was overvalued and in a "bubble"—i.e., at a price level well above value based purely on economic fundamentals. Global interest rates were starting to rise, especially in the US to defend the value of the dollar. Coming onto the scene in the early 1980s, computerized trading that applied advanced mathematical algorithms was something new and disruptive. (On Black Monday's twenty-fifth anniversary, Christopher Matthews wrote in TIME Magazine that at the time, observers estimated that as much as 70% of all trades made on any given day were initiated by computers executing high-frequency trading algorithms). Portfolio insurance using stock index futures was introduced to hedge portfolios against market declines. (Index investing and hedging with futures are now commonplace). It was also in the 1980s that stock markets around the world became deeply interconnected, which turned the '87 crash into the first simultaneous global phenomenon. (Though this was a new concept then, global crashes are no longer unexpected).

In the US, markets actually began to unravel the week before. The Fed reports that on the prior Friday, October 16, the DJIA lost 4.6%, in a 108-point decline, which was the largest one-day drop in its history in terms of points. Then followed the 508-point drop on Monday, for a combined 26% crash in two successive trading sessions. Where was the bottom? Over the same period, New Zealand's stock market collapsed by 60%; is that where we were headed? According to the Fed, traders around the world were literally racing each other to the pits to sell.

The Federal Reserve, under chairman Alan Greenspan, responded by providing cash to the 10 largest NY banks, which doubled their lending to securities firms; pouring liquidity into the system to generate demand has since become the Fed's stock response to financial crises and has come to be known as the "Greenspan put." Unlike many prior crashes, the sharp losses stemming from Black Monday were not followed by an economic recession or a banking crisis. In fact, stock markets quickly recovered. In just two trading sessions, the DJIA gained back 288 points, or 57%, of the total Black Monday downturn. Less than two years later, US stock markets surpassed their pre-crash highs. Anyone still invested breathed a sigh of relief.

But in the moment, investors and financial advisors found themselves flatfooted in the midst of a shocking negative surprise of unprecedented magnitude. They were unsure of how to respond to a "black swan" event. Popularized by Nassim Taleb in his book, *Fooled by Randomness,* a black swan is something you would simply never expect to see if you were raised in the northern hemisphere where all swans are white. Therefore, based on all the data and statistics you have at hand, you would never plan to see a black swan because you simply don't believe they exist. Statistically, the Crash of 1987 was a twenty standard-deviation event, which means mathematically, it should occur on average once every several billion years, i.e., practically never. It's an occurrence that can have huge impact, but is also so rare and improbable that it can't be computed, modeled or predicted.

Yet the Crash of 1987 did happen. I was there—and you may have been too. I remember, though you may have blocked it out. It's understandable. It was painful and traumatic, and the human ability to forget is a built-in survival mechanism. Investors, especially, tend to have a very selective memory, happily forgetting unpleasant losses. It was traumatic for me, too, but I can't forget. In fact, I make a point of remembering because I have a job to do—to help protect you from the negative financial consequences of such recurring events that are often exacerbated by your instinctual reaction to them. We were all much younger then. We're older now and don't have the luxury of time to recover portfolio losses, especially given the challenges we face as we spend down.

In retrospect, there was no need for panic. In fact, according to the follow-up Brady Presidential Task Force report, panic selling was estimated to have needlessly cost investors $1 trillion. But in the moment, facing a financial loss of unknown magnitude, fear overtook rational thought, statistical analysis, and probability modeling. Under severe stress, many investors tend to react irrationally—often to their own detriment.

Our Financial Ticks

Classical economic theory developed in the 18th Century proposed that human beings are rational, marginal-utility-seeking creatures who make financial decisions based on ice-cold calculation. But starting in the 1970s, a more contemporary school of economics emerged, focused on the study of measurable behavior when real people make real financial decisions. Working separately at Chicago, Princeton and UCLA, professors of psychology Richard Thaler, Daniel Kahneman and Shlomo Benarzi inaugurated the field of behavioral finance. Combining finance and behavioral science, its goal was to identify the emotional, psychological, and cognitive factors that shape real-time human financial choices in an effort to improve outcomes. For their contributions, both Kahneman and Thaler have been awarded Nobel Prizes in Economics.

The school of behavioral finance has emerged from their groundbreaking efforts to challenge the assumption of human rationality when it comes to money, and illuminates the complex inner workings of human decision-making, under both normal and stressful circumstances. The Nobel Prize-winning tenets of behavioral finance shed some light on the forces at work in shaping your financial mindset.

The theory starts from Kahneman's recognition of the roles emotion and intuition play in people's decision making. He proposed a framework of "two minds" to describe the way people make choices: the intuitive mind forms rapid judgments without conscious inputs, and the "reflective mind" is slow, analytical and requires conscious effort.

Financial advisors engage the reflective mind when they sit you down to calculate a retirement framework based on your risk profile, current circumstances, and future goals. But many decisions you make are often the products of your intuitive mind, and they are usually powerful enough to override any attempt by the reflective mind to temper or change them.

The problem is that the intuitive mind is susceptible to cognitive distortions attributable to built-in mental shortcuts, or biases, that frame how we perceive and process information. As a result, our impulses can be misguided, and our decisions can lead to calamitous effects. Aware or not of our cognitive biases, we are their prisoners. They're like ticks. We have no conscious control over them. In fact, *they* control *us*.

When it comes to our finances, fear of loss—loss aversion—is said to be at the core of our biases, dominating our decision-making and behavior. Scientific studies have shown that people display a hyper-negative response to potential loss in all its forms. Research conducted at Harvard found that for the average person, losses hurt twice as much as equivalent gains yield pleasure. Researchers at Columbia concluded that retirees are up to five times more sensitive to losses than the average person, so for the people reading this book, losses hurt ten times more than equivalent gains give pleasure!

Loss aversion renders people reluctant to change because they are more focused on what they could lose than on what they might gain, resulting in "inertia" and demonstrating what practitioners in the field call "status quo" bias. Retirees have been shown to view handing over control of their money (or the ability to access it whenever they want) as a form of loss. Studies have even shown that Americans fear outliving their money—i.e., losing access to it forever—more than they fear death itself!

Losses bring pain; gains bring pleasure. In dealing with loss aversion and the associated regret, people have the tendency to weigh losses significantly more heavily than gains. For example, investors tend to hold on to losing stocks too long because selling brings on loss recognition; by the same token, they often sell winning stocks too soon, because the sale realizes a gain and provides the attendant pleasure. Both trading choices are irrational and self-defeating, but the intuitive biases and emotional needs they satisfy simply overwhelm the reflective mind.

At the other end of the impulse-spectrum lies greed, the human desire for "more." In his 2004 Chairman's Letter, Warren Buffett, considered an investment oracle, advised that "the fact that people will be full of greed, fear or folly is predictable" so if investors insist on trying to time their participation in equities, they "should try to be fearful when others are greedy and greedy only when others are fearful." This was Buffett's acknowledgment that individual investors tend to buy high and sell low precisely because they follow the herd instead of taking a contrarian position. After loss aversion, *herding* is acknowledged to be the key bias at the root of average investor under-performance. Investors following the herd have historically bought high (out of greed) and sold low (out of fear).

The record shows that when the S&P 500 Index has performed well, there was an influx of money to equity funds (buying high); when the market pulled back, investors withdrew their money from equity funds (selling low) and rushed into fixed income (bond) funds. According to the legendary Buffett, plunging into rising markets and fleeing when markets fall is precisely the opposite of what investors should do to win at Wall Street's game. But financial behaviorists have explained why we just can't help it.

Nature built us to flee from predators, not to time markets— although some of our biases may try to persuade us otherwise. Take *overconfidence*, for example, a bias that leads people to believe they can outperform the market, and its associated *over-optimism*, a risk-seeking bias fed by prior success. All these adverse investor "ticks" are exacerbated by proven *short-sightedness*, a *recency bias* that inclines us to expect current trends to continue, and an *anchoring bias*, expressed as a tendency to chase performance based on the expectation that future outcomes will reflect past experience (despite all warnings about the unreliability of historic trends plastered everywhere throughout the financial industry).

The herding bias—the tendency for human beings to conform their behavior to the majority and to (foolishly) rely on the wisdom of the crowd—reflects our need for acceptance and confirmation.

Confirmation bias is a major driver of the psychological investing cycle, illustrated below:

FIGURE 17. THE UPS AND DOWNS OF INVESTOR PSYCHOLOGY HAVE REAL-TIME EFFECTS

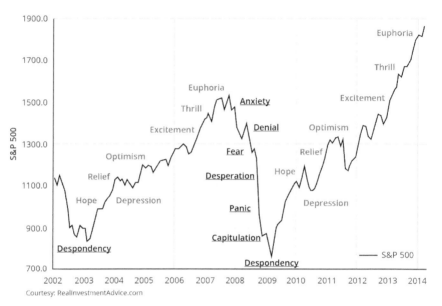

Courtesy: RealInvestmentAdvice.com

Confirmation bias also inclines us to "cherry pick" our information, listening only to what we want to hear. The media understand our need for validation, and in their efforts to please advertisers by attracting readers, listeners and viewers, they often frame the news and opinions they voice to confirm what we already (want to) believe, rather than present a raft of contrarian views and alternative insights.

Framing is the key to knowing and choosing. As human beings we constantly take in streams of sensory stimuli. Our minds filter the raw data and "frame it" into a picture of reality. Using language, we name things, relate them to each other, and formulate knowledge and beliefs about our model of the world. Whether providing or receiving information, once the raw data has been processed, it has been subjectively framed. But does the information reflect reality? Can we human beings even know what's "real"?

DM Syndrome

Leading up to Black Monday, investors framed their perception of the world in a version of *disaster myopia*. They operated from a position of excessive optimism, assuming that financial markets would continue to produce impressive positive returns in perpetuity. Investors were self-confident after seeing their wealth grow and tethered themselves to the expectation that future results would replicate past performance. A herd of baby boomers had thundered into the stock market, providing each other confirmation that it was the smart thing to do. Their frame of reference had no room for low-probability/high-magnitude events that were outside their individual experience, events that were basically unimaginable.

In fact, the coming crash was practically unforeseeable. It was a black swan event that defied probability analysis and was therefore impossible to predict. Unlike risk, the likelihood and effects of which can be measured, a black swan event embodies "Knightian uncertainty." First described by economist F.H. Knight in 1922, uncertainty cannot be measured in terms of probabilities. Its outcomes can neither be predicted, nor its effects known.

Faced with uncertainty, investor confidence is undermined relative to expectations about risk and return. Increasingly fearful, investors imagine adverse outcomes in the extreme and flock to the exits. In this scenario, risk assets quickly lose value as buyers and liquidity disappear. Panic in the face of Knightian uncertainty thus leads people to behave as though the likelihood of a catastrophe is much higher than it may actually be, at least in the absence of the panic itself. Panic feeds on itself in the form of negative confirmation. People now frame a given situation in terms of *disaster magnification*, a mental state of extreme pessimism in which the worst possible outcome is seen on the horizon.

What is the tipping point? Most often, it's a negative surprise, a shock, or an unforeseen change in the market or economic environment that turns mere risk into uncertainty, disaster myopia into disaster magnification.

For a financial advisor, managing assets can be much easier than managing clients in need of support in the face of market havoc. Specialists in behavioral finance designed 401(k) enhancements that successfully encouraged people to save more in their 401(k) plans. They explain that the key to their success as program designers is mechanistic simplicity, a built-in set-it-and-forget-it mechanism that, once operational, requires no thought or effort.

Obviously, managing people's innate behavioral response to a black swan event that is perceived to threaten financial ruin is a problem of a different order that evokes maximum loss aversion, extreme irrationality and desperate flailing. Some academics argue that better financial education can enhance investor savvy and strengthen investor resolve to stay invested through market downturns rather than rush for the exits. But they're effectively proposing that the reflective mind should be trained to overrule the intuitive mind and, having been in the trenches, this seems highly unrealistic. Others press for deepening the advisor-client relationship to enhance confidence in professional advice to stay the course in down markets (to assure eventual participation in the inevitable recovery). But I've found that, bottom line, clients don't like losing money, and when the pain of loss reaches a threshold of -15% or more, it's extremely difficult to keep them invested (and I'm not sure it's always a good idea).

Personally, I suffer from a version of what I call "DM Syndrome'—of the magnification variety—and try as I might, I can't shake it. Black Monday left an indelible mark on me. Knowing that the circuit breakers installed into the stock market's trading rules after the 1987 crash only limit a one-day index drop to 20%, I ask myself every morning if this might be the day the unforeseeable bears down on us. Apparently, I am not alone. Writing in the New York Times on Black Monday's 30th anniversary, Nobel Prize-winning Yale economist Robert Shiller opined that "we are still at risk (of a repeat of the worst day in stock market history)...because fundamentally that market crash was a mass stampede set off through viral contagion...(reflecting) a powerful narrative of impending market decline already embedded in many minds." In other words, the primary cause of Black Monday, according to Professor Shiller's research, was not financial or economic in nature. It was a shift in mass psychology fed by rumors gone viral (and that was before we had the Internet to instantly transmit them around the world).

Unlike in 1987, today I am prepared. And I believe my clients are also better prepared to weather market uncertainty, extreme volatility and even a sudden shift in mass psychology. Because the FIA anchoring the stable-core portfolio helps insulate investors from market losses, it can obviate panic, mitigate fear, prevent needless selling, and thankfully, help avoid recriminations. Investors in the FIA-anchored stable-core portfolio can stay calm and clear-sighted, their reflective minds in better control over their intuitive urges. But getting to that balance requires a degree of self-awareness and a good measure of conscious effort.

Your Mental Reset

FIGURE 18. WHAT CAN YOU SEE?

Consider Figure 18, known in Gestalt psychology as Ruben's vase. What do you see? Depending on your perceptual biases, you might see a white vase on a black background. Or do you see two black profiles facing each other on a white background? What image do you see first? Which comes naturally, the black figures on the white background or the white figure on the black background? Which one is real, and which is the optical illusion?

Isn't it interesting that the brain gives perceptual dominance to only one of these images at a time? We don't see both simultaneously. Moreover, you may see only one and not the other unless you look at it for a long time or make a strenuous mental effort to find the second image. This is how our mind works: it frames raw data and shapes it into what we often insist is a picture of reality, but that reality reflects our ingrained biases about what we put in the foreground and what we unconsciously relegate to the background. The narrative we accept about what's real and what's not, what's primary and what's secondary, shapes our mental view of the world.

In retirement planning and portfolio construction today, most advisors and clients put investment securities in the foreground of their mental picture, relegating guaranteed insurance products to a lesser role (if any) in the background. The stable-core portfolio reverses this perceptual framework. This poses a challenge: Putting insurance in the foreground calls for a cognitive reset that requires considerable mental effort to wrestle out from under the predominant framing constantly reinforced by the "retirement investing" narrative that has come to dominate public discourse.

FIGURE 19. THE INVESTOR LIFECYCLE

BUY THE HIGHS
Based on the fear of missing out

The Investor Life Cycle

SELL THE LOWS
Based on the fear of further losses

Courtesy: Core Income

Thus, achieving mastery over the investor life cycle illustrated in Figure 19 requires us to tame some of the most powerful psychological forces shaping our habitual financial behaviors. But internal forces are not the only ones that can upset our equilibrium. There are external forces as well, and we must see them for what they are.

Takeaways

1. The school of behavioral finance illuminates the complex inner workings of our minds when it comes to managing our money under both normal and stressful conditions.

2. Individuals' decision-making is influenced by built-in behavioral biases that often overwhelm rationality and thereby undermine investment success.

3. When markets turn back, fear-driven loss aversion can distort rational thinking and test our resolve.

4. The need for confirmation leads the average investor to buy high, while the dread of bottomless losses induces the average investor to sell low.

5. According to research firm Dalbar, buying high and selling low is believed to account for the 50% return shortfall suffered by average mutual fund investors when compared to the long-term average performance of the funds themselves.

Questions for your financial advisor

1. Where were you on Black Monday, what were its underlying causes, and do you think it could happen again?

2. What was the worst market crash (peak to trough) you and your clients have ever endured?

3. How did the portfolio you're recommending weather that crash?

4. How exactly is your recommended retirement portfolio built to protect someone like me from a self-destructive emotional response to negative market events?

5. Will your approach keep me invested through thick and thin and protect me from my worst instincts?

Chapter 5

THE MONEY MAKERS

Central banks launched the huge social experiment
of quantitative easing (QE) with carelessly
little thought about the side effects.

William White, PhD
Ex-Chief Economist, Bank for International Settlements

When Rob earned his second doctoral degree at UC Berkeley in the late 1960s and launched his international consulting career, he didn't expect to end up overseeing millions of British pounds spent to police trading traffic in the City of London. With degrees in process design, information systems and mathematics, he spent his earlier career living in Asia, Europe and the US working as a management consultant for non-financial corporations and high-tech startups. But after the Global Financial Crisis (GFC), although nearing retirement age, Rob was called to a new role: he was drafted into service as a global banking executive. Currently employed by some of the biggest financial institutions in the world, Rob now finds himself responsible for the design and implementation of immensely complex computer systems dedicated to one essential function: supervising international financial transactions to assure their compliance with ever-evolving regulatory demands imposed by the world's banking authorities in Brussels and Washington, DC.

That's because in the aftermath of the GFC, governments and regulators have recognized that banking practices were not incidental to the global crisis that almost crashed the world into an economic depression; the failings of a fragile global banking system were at its heart. Indeed, a more accurate account of events might depict a "Global Banking Crisis." So, after 2008, managing "systemic" banking risk became the focus, containing it became the goal, and internal compliance departments burgeoned, while equity, fixed-income and commodities trading desks shrank. Banking processes and culture came under the spotlight and the picture that emerged wasn't pretty. Many observers were shocked to learn that high-powered bankers were rigging global financial markets. Rob was tasked with building the systems that monitored for that kind of malfeasance and oversaw the banking equivalent of a self-regulating department of internal affairs.

Protected and Privileged

Criticized for brazen self-dealing, elitist privilege and even criminal misconduct, banking culture has come under increasing scrutiny since the Great Financial Crisis. For malfeasance ranging from manipulating the London Interbank Offered Rate (LIBOR) at which banks lend to each other and to which $800 trillion in global assets are pegged, to price-fixing Credit Default Swaps (CDS), to precious metals and energy trading, dozens of the biggest American and European banks have been fined for restraining competition via secret meetings held by traders to benefit themselves and their institutions.

Years of scandal and allegations of misconduct have taken a serious toll. Battered by an unending barrage of revelations, Americans' confidence in banks stood at 27% in a June 2016 Gallup Poll, well below the 40% historical average. Whether liberal or conservative, only one in four Americans were willing to say they had "a great deal or quite a lot" of confidence in banks, a level that is unchanged since 2013.

Nevertheless, it's no exaggeration to say that big banking remains a protected industry and high-powered bankers comprise a privileged elite. Why are we, the people, so forgiving? What exactly do banks contribute to our economy that renders them so essential?

Banks Make Money

American folk hero Willie Sutton may have put his finger on it. When asked back in the 1930s why he robbed banks, Sutton explained he did it because that was where the money could be found. How true: the large banks serve as the repository for the money that greases the wheels of commerce—the wellspring of our prosperity and standard of living—while they manage the global payment system that enables willing buyers and sellers around the world to transact business.

But that was a simpler time. Sutton was referring only to the currency sitting in the vaults and behind the teller windows. Currency is only one form of money. There are others that aren't as readily understood that only banks can create—and destroy—exercising an unlimited power that imbues them with an awesome hold on our lives, in what some have described as an age of unprecedented "financialization."

At its core, modern banking is the business of lending. Banks fill the role of financial intermediary between borrowers and savers. From its inception in the Middle Ages to serve the gold trade— storing, lending and issuing banknotes representing deposits held of the precious metal—bank lending was ingeniously built around other people's money (OPM). More than on their personal capital, the process relied on bankers' know-how, network and finesse. Rather than putting their own money at risk, bankers borrowed from savers (paying them a fee for the time the bank held custody of the money) and lent those "deposits" to borrowers (who paid an even higher fee for use of the money), earning their compensation and profit from the spread.

Sound banking practices would have dictated that a banker kept a 100% reserve against demand deposits, holding an ounce of gold in the vault for every one-ounce banknote issued. But bankers realized that they could lend a multiple of all the gold money deposited by their lenders by creating a multiple of banknotes against the same reserves, then keeping 100% of the interest charged on the overage. This was akin to lending the same gold bar ten or twenty times. This practice introduced leverage into the lending process; leverage compounded earnings, making banking very profitable.

But leverage also compounded risk, because it meant that available (liquid) reserves might fall to only a fraction of what depositors could actually demand. What has since become known as "fractional reserve" banking—lending a multiple of deposits on hand and holding only a fraction of what could be demanded by depositors at any one time—increased the risk of a run on the bank by panicked depositors all demanding their money at the same time. This scenario could force a bank to default and close its doors—causing havoc in the broader economy if it meant calling in previously extended loans.

US financial history is littered with banks that failed due to a mismatch of fractional reserves to depositor claims when poor judgment and/or bad business conditions caused losses from non-performing loans. This is what happened during the great banking panics of 1893, 1899 and 1907. And it's exactly what happened during the Great Depression. According to the Historical Statistics of the United States, between 1929 and 1933 some 10,000 banks (40% of all those in operation) closed their doors, ruining millions of unprotected depositors who simply could not get to their money. The banks had over-stretched during the "credit boom" of the Roaring '20s as they lent to unstable European nations recovering from WWI, to America's farmers investing in modernization to meet European demand for food, and to the investor class growing richer from the booming bull market fueled by stocks bought on "margin."

Margin buying was a form of leverage: a fraction of a stock's price was paid in investor cash that was then supplemented by funds lent by the banks and their brokerage affiliates, who were happy to use the underlying stock as collateral. Speculating with borrowed funds ratcheted up demand for equities, driving their prices to all-time highs, forming a bubble that gave off an aura of invincibility. The credit boom and inflated stock market fostered the illusion of a robust economy, masking the earnings stagnation suffered by many farmers and industrial workers; aggregate demand was in fact weakening. But analysts and politicians dismissed doomsday scenarios based on the un-sustainability of a constantly rising stock market, arguing that the US had entered a "new era," in which stock values and prices would always go up.

The stock bubble collapse in 1929 and ensuing margin calls led to the liquidation of $20 billion of bad bank loans extended during the previous debt bubble, about half of which ($9 billion) was stock market margin loans. This liquidation was followed from 1931 to 1933 by four waves of bank runs. The bank runs exacerbated a vicious cycle of business failures and defaults by causing some banks to call in loans that may have been performing. According to UCLA economist and Depression Era expert Christina Romer, at the bottom in 1934 this unwinding of debt culminated in a 25% unemployment rate. (By then, another 25% of breadwinners had already had their wages and hours cut, resulting in almost one out of every two US households directly experiencing either unemployment or underemployment). At its 1934 trough, the economic contraction was measured by a 47% collapse in industrial production, a 30% drop in real GDP, a 33% decrease in wholesale prices ("deflation") and a 31% drop in the money supply. As standards of living fell precipitously here and around the world, the traumatic impact was terrible human suffering, explains Professor Romer, leading to the social ferment and global political upheaval that ultimately triggered WWII.

The Unintended Consequences for Retirees

It's critically important to understand how bank policies and actions can adversely affect retirees. Under an economic system fueled by credit, the US and its citizens are indebted like never before. As of 2016, total government and personal debt stood at $33 trillion, most of which was accumulated over the last forty years. In 1980 the debt aggregate was about $3 trillion, of which government debt stood at less than $1 trillion. Today, the US national debt stands at $21 trillion after almost doubling over the last eight years alone. According to the US Department of the Treasury, at the current rate, federal debt could double to $40 trillion by 2030—assuming that trillions in private and government pensions don't implode and need to be bailed out by the federal government, thereby taking on even more debt in the process.

According to MarketWatch, by the end of 2016 Americans carried more debt (including consumer debt, mortgages, auto loans and student loans) than before the financial crisis. As US incomes have remained stagnant for decades, we've substituted debt for earnings in what some have come to call "debt-serfdom."

How might all this debt affect you? First, you may carry mortgage or educational debt (your children's or grandchildren's) and/or consumer obligations into retirement. Second, you may have to contend with a significant rise in the real cost of living during your retirement years, an inevitable byproduct of the Federal Reserve's tireless money creation. Third, as a saver, the Fed's zero-rate policy will challenge you to earn a safe return on your cash. Finally, as an investor, you may face decades of low returns—nominal and real—driven by slow growth in the underlying economy, and exacerbated by a little-understood process known as "financial repression."

Here is a snapshot of how we got into this predicament, and what it means for your retirement planning.

Banks Intermediate Financial Instability

It was in their central role as financial intermediaries that the banks transmitted the impact of the 1929 stock market collapse into the broader economy, helping to turn that crash into the worst economic contraction in American history. Challenged to respond to widespread desperation, governments everywhere felt it was their duty to act.

In the formerly laissez-faire US, the growing role of the central government in economic planning and market regulation gained wider acceptance. Economic regulation of the financial markets took off, and in 1935 unemployment compensation and old age and survivors insurance were initiated through the Social Security Act, planting the seeds of the welfare state.

The Great Depression shifted the focus of economic theory and monetary policy toward moderating the ebbs and flows of the business cycle. Today, governments and central banks around the world see their roles as active planners working together to moderate economic downturns and stimulate growth. In 1934, declining business and consumer spending led British economist John Maynard Keynes to argue that increases in government spending were necessary to make up for the resulting slack in economic activity. In the mid-1960s Milton Friedman and Anna Schwartz, leaders of the Monetarist School of Economics taught at the University of Chicago, focused policy attention on the money supply as the key determinant of economic prosperity. They went so far as to argue that the real cause of the Depression was monetary contraction, and that Federal Reserve policy errors during the 1930s actually made things worse, killing off a 9%-a-year GDP recovery that Professor Romer explains had been underway since 1934!

Thanks to Keynes, Friedman and Schwartz, the importance of the relationship between government spending and money supply policy has become economic consensus. Professional economists, central bankers and government officials now agree that never again should governments and banking authorities passively allow (or proactively foster) another economic depression. The wide acceptance of this view was typified by President Nixon's 1971 statement when he cut the dollar loose from the gold standard, literally proclaiming "We're all Keynesians now." For our central bank—the Federal Reserve System—this is embodied in the presumption that the monetary policies it devises and implements can determine the parameters of our nation's economic wellbeing. Believing itself indispensable to centrally planned prosperity, and supremely confident in its know-how at the monetary controls (despite repeated financial crises, crashes and disruptions), central banking has lifted itself to a heightened sense of self-importance, infused with narrative-setting economic preeminence and political clout. The financial industry, including the media, hangs on its every word.

The bottom line? Investors need to recognize the potential risks imposed by a banking culture that serves its own purposes, but that is not particularly focused on the needs or future wellbeing of America's retirees.

The Federal Reserve System: Our Central Bank

With its unique blend of private and governmental characteristics, the Federal Reserve System had a far more modest purpose when it was first launched in 1913. It was originally designed to serve the public interest and maintain financial stability by heading off the recurrent financial panics that a less unified banking system had suffered previously. To do so, it would serve solely as a "banker's bank" by offering a discount window to its 6,000 member banks, to better utilize system-wide reserves. Simply put, the Federal Reserve would serve as the lender of last resort to commercial banks that presented good collateral and that needed liquidity (cash) to meet depositor demands.

Starting in the 1980s, the Fed began to grow into its much larger, current role as accommodating buyer of government debt and co-manager of the nation's economy. It was at this time that deficit spending took off to serve the Keynesian prescription that Washington had to continuously intervene in the national economy. The Federal Reserve System has since become a principal agent of government; by buying federal debt, it has enabled politicians to spend without taxing. Unlike all other central banks, however, and despite appearances, the Fed is not an agency *of* government. It is privately owned and operated by its member banks. While the chair and vice-chair of its Board of Governors are appointed by the President of the United States, approved by the Senate and required to testify twice a year before the House Banking Committee, its policy-making twelve-member Board of Directors, The Federal Open Market Committee, is actually answerable to no one and requires no pre-approval for any actions it takes. Or as the Fed explains on its website, "its decisions are made independently."

The complex product the central banking system offers is credit. Credit is first a measure of worthiness. It is also a byproduct of leverage because it is derived as a multiple of other people's savings. Above all, credit can be monetized; like currency, it is a form of money that has its own financial reality. Banks turn credit into money by issuing debt. The reality is that banking does not "print" money into being, it "lends" money into being. In an ingenious feat of financial engineering, banks create money when they lend wealth that they themselves have borrowed!

FIGURE 20. LENDING MONEY INTO EXISTENCE

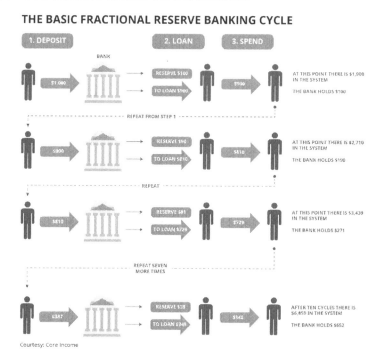

Courtesy: Core Income

In a fractional reserve system, the lending process can create money by a multiple of 10x to 20x their reserves, depending on the prevailing reserve requirement set by the Fed and the demand for credit. Conversely, when loans default, get repaid or are simply not made because of lack of demand, the total money supply is proportionately reduced. (Money grew scarce during the Great Depression because so many loans defaulted and so few new ones were made).

Debt

For lenders, sound debt is good and the more of it that is outstanding, the better. The good news for lenders is that these are
boom times for debt. According to data from the Institute of
International Finance, in Q3 2017 global debt reached $233 trillion,
over 318% of world GDP, amounting to the largest debt bubble in
history. How has it reached this size? Largely due to central bank
accommodation of Keynesian government spending during and after
the GFC-triggered recession, on the theory that central bank
purchases of government securities would reignite economic activity.

FIGURE 21. THESE ARE BOOM TIMES FOR GLOBAL INDEBTEDNESS

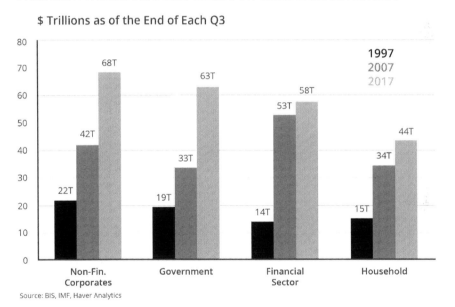

$ Trillions as of the End of Each Q3

Source: BIS, IMF, Haver Analytics

A disciple of Milton Friedman, Dr. Ben Bernanke was Fed
chairman in 2008. Like his mentor, he believed that the Great
Depression was *caused* by the Federal Reserve's failure to increase the
money supply during the 1930s. So, his response to the Great
Recession of 2008-09 was three rounds of Quantitative Easing (QE),

creating money to buy government and federal housing agency securities for the Fed's balance sheet, while releasing reserves to member banks at little to no cost. The reserves were expected to stimulate productive commercial lending at relatively low rates of interest (since the reserves making the loans possible were practically free) and enable the banking system to multiply money creation— through lending—to build up the money supply. By lending the Fed's reserves at practically no charge, Bernanke was increasing the member banks' deposit base, against which they could lend to credit-worthy customers to counteract the economic contraction that was underway.

Bernanke admitted that while Quantitative Easing was consistent with Monetarist theory, it was still only "an experiment," but central banks around the world still followed headlong and did the same. The one exception was the Bank of Japan, which had already begun its own version of QE in 2003 in response to the secular stagnation that previewed the effects of the Global Financial Crisis. Japan's QE had been of little avail; Bernanke criticized it then for being too hesitant, although it turned out that our own QE1, 2 and 3 also failed to achieve their intended GDP growth effects.

Integral to loosening the money supply and making loans cheap, Bernanke initiated ZIRP, the Zero Interest Rate Policy. ZIRP set the interest rates over which the Federal Reserve had control at close to zero. These were the Discount Rate on loans made to member banks borrowing reserves and the Fed Funds rate on overnight loans made between banks to meet overnight reserve and capital requirements. Essentially, Bernanke declared that "helicopter money" would fall from the skies to be gathered up (nearly for free) by prime borrowers, such as major corporations, and the bankers and financiers who had first access to it.

Unfortunately, these rates also set benchmarks for interest paid on customer deposits, driving rates down to a pittance and crushing your savings' earning power. In Bernanke's crusade to save the world from the next Depression, the financial fortunes of risk-averse retirees would have to be sacrificed—and their tolerance for risk challenged—for the good of big-time economic actors who could continue to borrow and spend.

Financial Bubbles

By applying ZIRP to the government securities issued by the US Treasury to fund its deficit spending, the Fed could theoretically deliver huge multiplier effects to the broad economy. It bid, and the US Treasury accepted, very low rates on that debt, driving down the cost of government borrowings. Because US Government bills, notes and bonds are denominated in the US dollar and set the standard for "risk-free" investing, new US debt issues set the floor for all rates on public and private debt denominated in all currencies—reflecting the dollar's international reserve status. So, by effectively setting the rates on US government paper, Bernanke was able to suppress the yields on fixed-income instruments of all types around the world.

Governments have been borrowing on the cheap—and investors have been chasing yield—ever since. One key byproduct of ZIRP: at last count a $63 trillion bubble in sovereign debt, the borrowings of the world's governments, comprising perhaps the next bubble to burst. A secondary bubble: overvalued stocks that trade based on bond yields: the lower the bond yields fall, the higher stock prices rise.

But where would the Fed get the money to buy the Government's offerings? The Federal Open Market Committee couldn't increase reserve requirements to raise cash from member banks, as calling in reserves would reduce liquidity, raise interest rates and slow economic activity—the opposite of the Fed's intended mission. Designed to be the lender of last resort and with no others to tap, the Federal Reserve did the only thing it could: it created the money it needed from thin air. The Fed bought government obligations with the press of a button, electronically crediting the government's accounts with the purchase price it offered. It effectively created money from nothing, and put it at the disposal of the US government.

FIGURE 22. THE FEDERAL RESERVE BALANCE SHEET

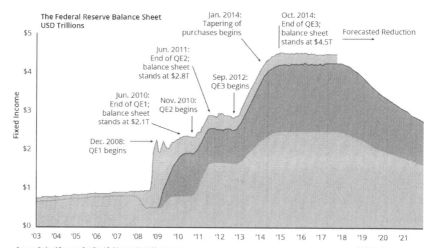

Source: Federal Reserve, FactSet, J.P. Morgan Asset Management.
Currently, the balance sheet contains $2.5 trillion in Treasuries and $1.8 trillion in MBS. The end balance forecast is $1.6 trillion in Treasuries and $1.1 trillion in MBS. *Balance sheet reduction assumes reduction from current level, beginning October 2017 until December 2021. Reduction of Treasuries and MBS is per FOMC guidelines from the September 2017 meeting minutes: the cap on Treasury securities will begin at $6 billion month initially and reduction rate will increse in steps of $6 billion at three-month intervals over 12 months until reaching $30 billion per month; the MBS cap will begin at $4 billion per month initially and will increase in steps of $4 billion at three-month intervals over 12 months until reaching $20 billion per month; Other asstes are reduced in proportion. In those months where the amount of maturing assets do not exceed the stated cap then the balance sheet will be reduced by the total amount of maturing assets. *Guide to the Markets - U.S.* Data are as of December 31, 2017

J.P.Morgan
Asset Management

Figure 22 shows that since the start of the QE process in 2008, the Fed's "balance sheet" has grown from $500 billion to $4.5 trillion in 2017, or about nine-fold. It holds US Treasury securities, agency debt and Mortgage Backed Securities (MBS), Repurchase Agreements and Central Bank Liquidity Swaps—not exactly your everyday financial assets. The complexity of its domestic operations, its global reach and its centrality to money supply around the world often requires the Fed to take extraordinary steps it feels are necessary, with no obligation to disclose or justify its actions to the American public. Examples include the emergency loans of $1.6 trillion to unnamed American banks at the height of the crisis in December 2008, the billions in Foreign Exchange (FX) swaps that year to keep the world's central banks supplied with dollars, and the billions in excess interest currently paid to big foreign banks on their US dollar reserves.

Sometimes it might even seem that the Fed's interest-rate setting and market-price manipulations could serve as a model for those trading practices that went over the line at some of its owner banks. In terms of its unconstrained attitude, insider access, burgeoning asset portfolio and one-hundred-fold leverage, some observers think it's starting to look like a hedge fund. And like a hedge fund, its strategies can be convoluted and opaque.

Wealth Inequality

Federal Reserve liquidity—in the form of cheap credit for the wealthy—has inflated financial asset bubbles in stocks and bonds that have further enriched the already-concentrated top 5% of the wealth pyramid. Owning over 70% of all financial assets, the top 5% also comprise the only segment of households that registered gains in real income over the last twenty years, according to the US Census Bureau and G. William Domhoff, author of "Wealth, Income and Power."

FIGURE 23. THE DISTRIBUTION OF WEALTH IN THE US SINCE 1917

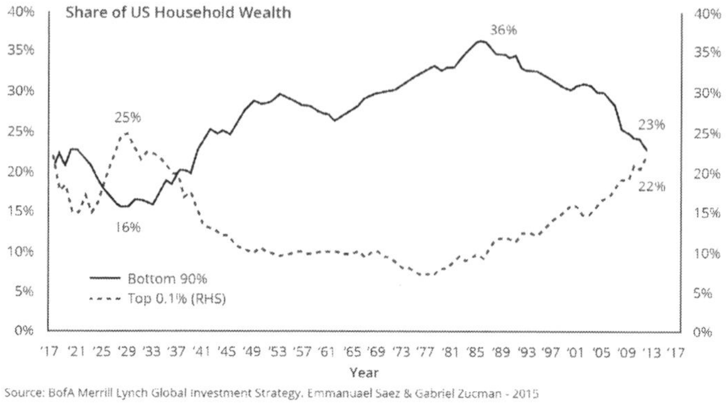

Source: BofA Merrill Lynch Global Investment Strategy, Emmanuael Saez & Gabriel Zucman - 2015

By favoring the wealthy, specifically the banker and financier class, central bank policies have widened income and wealth inequality to extremes not seen since the Great Depression. Figure 23 shows that as of 2015, the top 0.10% of US households owned as much wealth as the bottom 90%. A report based on the Federal Survey of Consumer Finances by economist Edward N. Wolff released in late 2017 revealed that the wealthiest 1% of American households own 40% of the country's wealth, a higher share than at any point since at least 1962. With the gap between the ultra-wealthy and everyone else growing ever wider, at least over the past few decades, it seems fair to deduce that central bank policies have been an unqualified success for both bankers and financiers, and their prime borrowers.

Thus, it can be argued that the Fed has not only failed to rectify the nation's inequality in wealth and income, it has actually widened it by handing guaranteed returns on free money to the banking sector while eviscerating non-labor income by crushing the interest paid on savings. Rather than stimulating economic recovery that trickled down to the working classes to achieve widely shared prosperity, QE and ZIRP have supplied limitless, nearly free money to the banking sector to generate risk-free profits.

Real Inflation

Creating money out of nothing and pouring it into the financial system is the very essence of "inflation," defined as "an increase in the quantity of money." The direct effect of inflation, of course, is the erosion of monetary purchasing power: more dollars chasing the same amount of goods drives prices higher, and a given amount of currency ends up buying less. Despite its initial primary purpose—to promote financial stability and preserve the purchasing power of the dollar—in fact, the Federal Reserve System has overseen a 95% erosion of the dollar's value as a medium of exchange. Insisting on achieving 2% annual inflation as an economic policy goal implies further depreciation in purchasing power over the coming decades.

So why, after the introduction of trillions of fiat dollars into the system, is consumer price inflation so low today?

Calculated by the government's Bureau of Labor Statistics (BLS) since 1917, the Consumer Price Index for Urban Consumers (CPI-U) released in June 2017 put the year-over-year inflation rate at 1.87%, less than half its 3.77% average since the end of the WWII and just above its 10-year moving average, at this writing, of 1.76%. The Fed was not satisfied, insisting that a target inflation rate of at least 2% per year must be met to sustain economic recovery and improve employment figures. Calling for more inflation may seem to contradict the Fed's mandate to preserve price stability, but it gives precedence to its faith in the Phillips Curve, which links higher inflation to improved employment prospects.

The Consumer Price Index was initiated during World War I when prices were rising rapidly, making it essential to have an index for calculating cost-of-living adjustments for wages. Beginning in the 1980s, its method of calculation started to change with the introduction of statistical and qualitative measures. Since then, those changes may have saved the federal government hundreds of billions in cost-of-living-adjusted benefit payouts.

But today, the result is that the CPI fails to measure a simple basket of goods that consumers typically purchase, which was its original intent. Instead, it weights the items in the official basket to reduce the impact of higher priced ones and "games" quality improvements to overstate their effects. In other words, the case can be made that the official inflation rate is a statistical methodology divorced from real people's lives. In response, a growing school of experts (using the original measures for calculating rises in the cost of living) have reached a consensus CPI rate of 8% over the last ten to twenty years.

FIGURE 24. CONSUMER INFLATION: OFFICIAL VS SHADOWSTATS (1980-BASED)

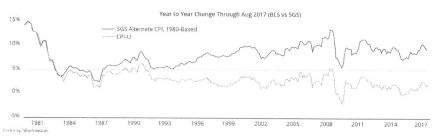

Utilizing an inflation rate of 8% over the last twenty years instead of the generally accepted rate of less than 3% undermines a fundamental assumption shaping our economic narrative: Applying an 8% average inflation rate to nominal GDP growth since 2009 would mean negative real economic growth in the range of -6% per annum, implying a prolonged recession (if not depression) rather than a recovery since the GFC.

An 8% inflation rate would also drive "real" interest rates into deeply negative territory. If the cost of living is indeed rising at 8%, an annual 3% nominal long-term government bond yield would deliver a 5% *loss* in real purchasing power, a miserable result for risk-averse investors and retirees trying to sustain their standard of living. Anything in the range of a negative real return on fixed income assets would compromise capital preservation, distort portfolio allocation, and crush performance. Forget about getting ahead or even keeping up, in a low-yield/high-inflation environment you would fall further behind each passing year, growing poorer as the dollars in your pocket (or your bank account) depreciate and buy less.

The Debt/GDP Ratio

The Fed's purchases of Treasury obligations have pushed our publicly-held federal debt/GDP ratio to over 100%, as shown in Figure 25. This means that today, the US government owes more to its creditors than the value of one full year of national economic productivity.

FIGURE 25. GROSS FEDERAL DEBT AS A % OF GDP

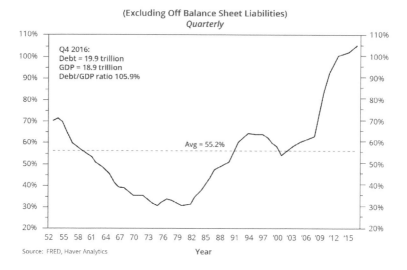

And the ratio is still climbing. According to a 2017 report from the Congressional Budget Office (CBO) that examined the long-term US economic outlook, the agency forecasts that government debt held by the public is expected to soar in the coming 30 years, driven primarily by Social Security and healthcare outlays expended on behalf of our growing elderly population. By 2047, the federal debt/GDP ratio is projected to reach 150% (Figure 26).

FIGURE 26. NATIONAL DEBT AS A GROWING FRACTION OF GDP

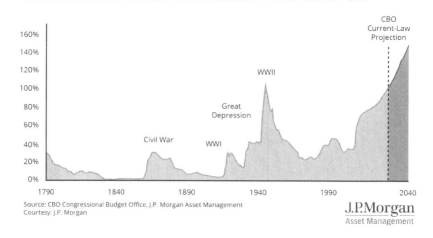

In other words, boomer retirement is expected to drive our national debt to unprecedented heights, greater than the debt generated by the Great Depression and even WWII!

Although the original intent was to accelerate economic activity, debt expansion hasn't worked (yet). As reported by the US Bureau of Economic Analysis, (through 2017) real GDP growth has averaged 1.6% since 2008, barely half our long-term GDP growth rate since 1947 (3.22%), despite the injection of trillions of federal dollars into the system.

Here's the rub: independent studies have shown that when the ratio surpasses 85%, government debt becomes a *drag* on growth. Perhaps the most noteworthy research on this critical subject was published in 2012 in the Journal of Economic Perspectives. In their seminal analysis, economists Carmen Reinhart and Kenneth S. Rogoff identified 26 cases of "debt overhangs"—defined as public debt/GDP ratios over 90% lasting for at least five years. On average, the authors found that these overhangs lasted for 23 years and, in almost all the instances, reduced economic growth by 1.2% annually compared to countries without comparable debt. The long duration of such episodes meant that the cumulative shortfall from the debt excess—23 years in a row of subpar economic growth—was potentially massive.

Economist Lacy Hunt has concluded that an extended period of debt/GDP ratio over 100% could mean that over the long term our economy will increasingly resemble Japan's. "(Japan's) public and private debt is just under 600% of GDP," he writes, and "our total public and private debt is about 373%. (Japan) has tried to solve (its) indebtedness problem by taking on more debt...but a study published in 2010 by the McKinsey Global Institute looked at 24 advanced economies that became extremely over-indebted and concluded that the longer-term trend in every case was to weaker and weaker economic performance…on the model of Japan's multi-decade stagnation."

The CBO report forecasts only 2% or less GDP growth over the next three decades. In the face of our aging demographics, rising healthcare costs and growing federal interest payments, it expects budget deficits to soar, requiring ever more debt that will further weigh down growth. A key problem here is that stock prices ultimately reflect real economic activity. As stock price increases depend on growth in revenues and profits, where will they come from in a stagnating economy?

Financial Repression

For over-indebted governments addicted to deficit spending, negative real returns are desperately needed. What a fortuitous coincidence for a spendthrift government that its politically-independent central banking system has determined that for the good of the country the time is right to set interest rates near zero, buy government securities with trillions created out of thin air, and keep any resulting consumer price inflation under the radar!

In doing so, the Federal Reserve System has provided government with the building blocks of "financial repression," a long-term process to which heavily indebted governments regularly resort when they need to reduce their debt/GDP ratio below the critical 90% threshold. Financial repression is one of four options to reduce the ratio. The others are (1) decades of consistent 4%+ economic expansion, which has thus far proven elusive; (2) debt default and restructuring that would undermine our nation's status as the risk-free standard; and (3) fiscal austerity requiring reduced spending and increased taxes (cf. Greece), which is not at all politically acceptable—especially by retirees. Though politically easy to implement because its effects are imperceptible as they gradually build, financial repression inflates away public debt by forcing real rates below GDP growth.

FIGURE 27. FINANCIAL REPRESSION CAN LAST A LONG TIME

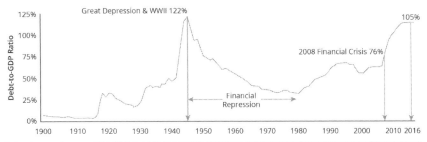

Past performance is no guarantee of future results. Sources: IMF, Datastream and Allianz Global Investors Economics & Strategy Group.

The process can take a long time, but it works. Figure 27 shows the last time the US resorted to financial repression starting in 1945, when the US debt-to-GDP ratio was 122%. It took 35 years, until 1980, to reduce the ratio to 30%, but by keeping real government yields below 1% for two-thirds of that time, the federal government was able to inflate away the enormous debt left over from the Great Depression and World War II.

How long will our next round of financial repression last? The process has to be slow to be imperceptible. A repeat of last century's experience would mean near-zero interest rates eroded by inflation for decades to come. But adverse demographics and slow economic growth could stretch the process even further. Recall that during the period from 1945-1980 we had the wind at our backs—thanks to the baby boom that stimulated economic growth—and it still took 35 years. This time we'll be repressing into an aging, shrinking population that is already showing signs of economic slowdown. In the 21st Century, will it take 50 years to get to a ratio of 30%?

The process of financial repression rewards debtors by enabling them to pay down their debts with cheapened dollars, while punishing savers by starving them of yield, eroding their purchasing power and forcing them to take uncomfortable risks to chase returns. In a near-ZIRP inflationary environment, cash is a wasting asset that has to be "securitized" to have any chance of preserving its purchasing power, let alone grow in value. But investing in securities requires taking on risk.

You're On Your Own

Available to the general public, every year the Federal Reserve publishes a statement of purpose entitled "Overview of the Federal Reserve System" in which it proclaims that "the Federal Reserve performs five key functions in the public interest to promote the health of the US economy and the stability of the US financial system." The Fed, it specifies:

> **Conducts the nation's monetary policy** to promote maximum employment, stable prices and moderate long-term interest rates in the US economy;
>
> **Promotes the stability of the financial system** and seeks to minimize and contain systemic risks;
>
> **Promotes the safety and soundness of individual financial institutions** and monitors their impact on the financial system as a whole;

Fosters payment system safety and efficiency through services to the banking industry and the US government; and

Promotes consumer protection and community development through consumer-focused supervision...and the administration of consumer laws and regulations."

Focused on these five extraordinarily complex mandates, the Fed clearly has its hands full. But isn't there something missing? Other than as a possible side effect of its other activities, the Federal Reserve System makes no pretense about shouldering a mandate to provide financial security to America's retirees. On the contrary, as we've seen, sometimes the unintended consequences of its policies can stand in direct conflict with the needs of retirees, such as when they starve them for yield and impel them to chase risk-on-returns.

And if it's returns you're looking for, then it's to the Wall Street subset of banking institutions that you must turn.

Takeaways

1. In today's financial world, bankers serve government borrowers, with both borrower and lender believing that national economic wellbeing depends on their collaborative market interventions.

2. As credit-issuers, the banks serve as intermediaries that leverage fractional reserves to stimulate economic activity by literally creating money through the lending process itself.

3. The Federal Reserve System, our "central bank," was established in 1913 to mitigate liquidity pressure on banks. After 10,000 banks still failed during the early phase of the Great Depression, the Federal Deposit Insurance Corporation (FDIC) was introduced to serve as an additional layer of depositor protection to tamp down the public's tendency to panic.

4. Some of the unintended consequences of modern banking practices include wealth inequality, monetary inflation, excessive debt burdens on households and governments and manipulated rates that favor borrowers at the expense of savers.

5. While the Fed sees its mandate today as protecting the international strength of the US dollar and interacting with our economy to help it achieve full employment and broad-based prosperity, our banking system does not shoulder a specific mandate to provide financial security to America's retirees and, in fact, some of its actions may actually prove inimical

Questions for your financial advisor

1. Why are rates at the bank so low that I can't earn enough on my cash to safely retire on the interest and preserve the principal for heirs?

2. What's the real inflation rate, especially for retirees whose predominant discretionary expenditures are for healthcare?

3. Do you think our debt-to-GDP ratio is too high, and will that affect my personal retirement planning in any way?

4. How will "financial repression" affect me, and what, if anything, can I do to counteract its consequences without creating even bigger problems for myself?

5. Do the big banks offer any products specifically designed to help risk-averse retirees meet their long-term income needs?

Chapter 6

WALL STREET INSECURITIES

Unless you have millions and millions and millions...

you cannot retire...on the investment return on your savings...

because there is no return on it.

Jeff Gundlach, Bond King & Modern Art Collector
Founder and CIO, DoubleLine Capital

I first conferred with Mauricio in 1995, overlooking New York's Central Park from a Fifth Avenue penthouse filled with modern art. Studying his experience as a do-it-yourself retiree has taught me an invaluable lesson: Even if you enter retirement with many millions, you are always subject to the risks, rules and ratios embedded in modern retirement planning. Should they go misunderstood or ignored, the result can be depletion and austerity—no matter how wealthy you may be starting out. Retirement success, on the other hand, especially if you have only modest wealth, depends on an informed approach to managing your nest egg that properly balances your capital and spending over an open-ended time horizon.

Do you find it hard to believe that even the very rich can run out of money? (Do you find it even harder to be sympathetic?) Allow me to demonstrate the vital lessons worth learning.

Deciding to enter retirement as he turned 65, Mauricio had just completed the sale of a Parisian fashion company he founded, clearing a nest egg of $100 million. Our purpose in meeting that day was to discuss his legacy planning. He faced a 50% estate tax upon his death and was looking for ideas that could mitigate the impact of those levies on his children and grandchildren. As for Mauricio's income planning, he wasn't looking for help from me or anyone else. He made it clear that he would consider only US Government bills, notes and bonds.

Mauricio, as it turns out, had serious trust issues. A Holocaust survivor, he spent some of his formative years in Buchenwald, the Nazi slave-labor camp near Weimar, Germany. At age 15, he was one of the prisoners liberated by American troops in April 1945. While maintaining his European connections and building a post-war business there, Mauricio became a proud and grateful American citizen, trusting in the inherent goodness and reliability of US government promises. It was simply unthinkable that the United States of America could ever default. In his mind, government paper was as safe as safe could be, and he viewed it as the key to a "risk-free" retirement that would let him sleep soundly at night while enabling him to live a fulfilling life by day.

And he wasn't one to fuss. A saver at heart, he'd be happy to buy and hold US notes for their ten-year duration and simply roll them over to new issues when they matured. He would hear of nothing else. Risk was anathema. Professional advice was gratuitous. He would manage his own money by lending it (safely) to the US Treasury.

Besides, in January 1995 savers like Mauricio could still thrive. The risk-free ten-year Treasury note was yielding 7.69%. In theory, it would pay him annual interest of $7,690,000 for ten years without having to dip into principal. What's more, that yield was tax-advantaged: interest income on US Government obligations was then (and is still) given preferential tax treatment. He would have to pay about 40% in federal income taxes but would avoid New York State and City taxes that together could have easily added another 10% or so to the burden.

Mauricio estimated that around $4.6 million spendable dollars would enable him to fund his family needs and essential living requirements, his discretionary globetrotting, his passion for modern art and his generous philanthropy. So, he matched his lifestyle to the income his capital would generate. "Living off the interest," he began his retirement by effectively withdrawing 7.97% from his nest egg. As for his estate-tax obligation, he would simply set up a life insurance trust and be done with it.

Later on, I learned that Mauricio had failed to factor in inflation, which averaged around 3% a year during the decade that followed (and even more in the prices bid for modern art). To keep up with his increasing cost of living he would have to up his annual withdrawal. To avoid dipping into principal, Mauricio faced the sacrifice of reducing his art-buying and charitable giving. He decided to give his lifestyle priority. Luckily, falling Fed interest rates during this period mitigated any capital depletion as he sold some of his bonds into a rising-price market. Still, after ten years, he found that he was left with only $85 million of the $100 million with which he began (Table 2).

When he rolled his portfolio over in 2005, however, 10-year rates on government notes had fallen to 4.16%. Reinvesting his capital at age 75, he would be earning $3.54 million in interest, less than half of what he had started with ten years earlier, and after federal income tax, it would leave just $2 million spendable dollars. Meanwhile, his annual expenses had inflated to over $10 million. Withdrawing $10 million a year from an $85 million nest egg would equate to a 12% annual withdrawal rate. Now 75, he wanted that money to last him another 25 years, just to be safe, and a 12% withdrawal rate would put him at great risk of premature depletion.

Facing the same challenge that can confront every retiree, Mauricio recognized that something had to give—despite the abundance with which he was blessed. He would either have to cut back his lifestyle or tap into principal and risk running out of money. He decided to reduce his annual withdrawal to $6.5 million. His art collecting slowed; his travels became less frequent; his charitable contributions less charitable. Bottom line: he started to feel pinched.

Despite the belt-tightening, at age 85 Mauricio found he only had $42.5 million remaining when the time came to replenish his matured portfolio with newly issued bonds. His luck couldn't have been worse. It was January 2015 when the ten-year rate hit 1.81% and Mauricio had to face the reality that his remaining principal would generate taxable interest of just $766,000 each year! Still healthy and active, he found himself a victim of his own loss-aversion, severely set back by the Fed's Zero Interest Rate Policy (ZIRP). His was an almost unbearable dilemma: Accept more austerity by further shrinking his lifestyle, family and charitable giving (and start to sell off his beloved art collection) and *still* face possible depletion at age 95—and/or chase higher yields by taking on more risk.

TABLE 2. MAURICIO'S SURPRISING RETIREMENT OUTCOME

Calendar Year	US 10-Yr	Starting Balance	Withdrawal 3% Inflation	End of Year Balance	
1995	0.2348	100,000,000	7,690,000	113,984,388	
1996	0.0143	113,984,388	7,920,700	107,580,399	
1997	0.0994	107,580,399	8,158,321	109,304,632	
1998	0.1492	109,304,632	8,403,071	115,956,075	
1999	-0.0825	115,956,075	8,655,163	98,448,587,	
2000	0.1666	98,448,587	8,914,818	104,450,095	
2001	0.0557	104,450,095	9,182,262	100,574,251	
2002	0.1512	100,574,251	9,457,730	104,893,339	
2003	0.038	104,893,339	9,741,462	98,767,648	
2004	0.0449	98,767,648	10,033,706	82,718,097	
2005	0.0287	91,718,097	10,334,717	84,747,783	
					Belt Tightening
2006	0.0196	84,747,783	6,500,000	79,781,439	
2007	0.1021	79,781,439	6,695,000	80,548,565	
2008	0.201	80,548,565	6,895,850	88,456,910	
2009	-0.1112	88,456,910	7,102,726	72,307,599	
2010	0.0846	72,307,599	7,315,807	70,490,098	
2011	0.1604	70,490,098	7,535,281	73,052,769	
2012	0.0297	73,052,769	7,761,340	67,230,584	
2013	-0.091	67,230,584	7,994,180	53,845,892	
2014	0.1075	53,845,892	8,234,006	50,515,164	
2015	0.0128	50,515,164	8,481,026	42,574,175	
					More Belt Tightening
2016	0.0069	42,572,175	4,100,000	38,737,633	
2017	0.028	38,737,633	4,223,000	35,481,043	
2018	0.025	35,481,043	4,349,690	31,909,637	
2019	0.025	31,909,637	4,480,181	28,115,192	
2020	0.025	28,115,192	4,614,586	24,088,121	
2021	0.025	24,088,121	4,753,024	19,818,475	
2022	0.025	19,818,475	4,895,614	15,295,932	
2023	0.025	15,295,932	5,042,483	10,509,785	
2024	0.025	10,509,785	5,193,757	5,448,929	
2025	0.025	5,448929	5,349,570	101,843	Proj. Depletion at Age 95

Source: 1995 - 2017 Professor Aswath Damodaran, PhD, NYU Stern School of Business. 2018 - 2025 projected returns at 2.5%.

A Shadow Banking Crisis

Mauricio's dilemma is the same one that has faced all savers since the Great Recession of 2008. Low yields pressure you to turn to a subset of "shadow banks" for greater returns.

Like the big commercial banks, the shadow banks are financial intermediaries. Unlike their commercial counterparts, they are not "cash depository" institutions; they are neither able to borrow from the Fed's discount window in a crisis nor insure your account for up to $250,000. Some of the shadow banks—the ones of interest to us as investors—specialize in the issuance, custody and trading of non-cash financial instruments known as stocks and bonds. These institutions include the investment banks, broker dealers, money management firms, mutual fund companies and hedge funds that comprise the Wall Street community.

The Wall Street subset of the shadow-banking universe provides no guarantees. On the contrary, like commercial banks they commerce in risk—offering returns arguably great enough to compensate for the possibility of "capital impairment," i.e., financial losses, temporary or otherwise. The Wall Street shadow banks earn money by exposing your cash to risk and trading their own.

At its heart, the Great Financial Crisis was really a shadow-bank seize-up triggered by some of Wall Street's biggest investment banks. It unfolded only after several years of huge profits reaped by the industry from the securitization of subprime mortgages into synthetic Mortgage Backed Securities (MBS). Rated Triple-A and sold aggressively to other institutional investors, the Wall Street mutual lending process froze up when the fraternity acknowledged the credit-quality story they were selling each other (and their customers) had significant holes. The seizure occurred in the overnight lending market. The Wall Street investment banks rely on overnight loans made between them to meet regulatory solvency requirements.

After running out of acceptable collateral, Lehman Brothers found itself at the epicenter of the crisis when it was deemed no longer worthy of overnight credit. Established in 1840 and the fourth largest investment bank in the United States, Lehman had gone "all in" to profit from every level of subprime mortgage issuance. It bought four mortgage originators to supply the loans to its derivatives specialists who chopped and diced them into tranches that earned the highest credit ratings, despite the subprime elements that were embedded within.

Lehman earned huge fees at every stage of the process and was leveraged about 40 to 1, meaning the bank had 2.5 cents in capital for every dollar of outstanding liability. That proved to be woefully insufficient capital to fall back on in a crisis. Like Bear Stearns and Merrill Lynch, Lehman held inventories of MBS and toxic real estate it priced at face value, and it used those securities as collateral when borrowing overnight from other banks on the Street. The crisis manifested when lenders began to question the true value of those securities and refused to accept them as collateral to avoid waking up the next morning holding the bag!

Not a member of the Federal Reserve System, and therefore unable to access the discount window, Lehman could look only to the US Treasury for capital. It was turned down. When it declared bankruptcy on September 15, 2008, with $600 billion in assets, Lehman Brother's was the largest bankruptcy filing in US history. With the entire global banking system at risk of collapse from contagion, the Fed Chair and US Treasury Secretary swung into action, and the rest is history.

Transforming Savers into Investors

The Wall Street retail value proposition purports to transform savers into investors by converting their spare cash into a form of money known as "securities." Securities come in a myriad of forms, but based on their fundamental properties, they turn individuals into either lenders or owners. Reduced to their essentials, securities take two basic forms: stocks, which reflect ownership of equity in a business enterprise, and bonds, which reflect an obligation owed to you by an enterprise to which you have lent funds. The yield that both stocks and bonds pay is a key determinant of their price. Here's what you need to understand about their underlying dynamics:

When buying a **bond**, you're lending money to a government or business in return for an interest payment over a given period of time, at the end of which you expect to be fully repaid. Like lending to a bank when you make a deposit, you are giving the borrower the use of your money for a price. Bonds come in a myriad of forms, offering claims against the borrower's assets in the event of default based on the specific terms of the loan set forth in their respective indentures. If a secured borrower defaults, you may claim against its assets for repayment and you may come before other types of creditors. The less risk incurred in making the loan—i.e., the more credit-worthy the borrower—the lower the interest offered. When held to maturity, the interest payments over time comprise your yield. Their steady cash flow stabilizes their value, so in terms of price, bonds tend to be less volatile than stocks.

Buying a share of **stock** represents an incident of ownership, or equity, in a business. Stocks have no maturity date; you own them until you decide to sell them. Their payouts come in the form of dividends made at the discretion of management—both in terms of magnitude and periodicity. Some years you may get more, some less, and some none depending on the company's operating profitability and other financial circumstances.

Among larger, mature dividend-paying US companies, dividends reflect about 50% of annual earnings. Dividend flow as a percent of the share price you paid is a critical component of stock ownership, sometimes amounting to 40% of the total return earned over time. But as an owner, you are taking the risk of total loss in the event of business failure because you are at the bottom of the capital stack, and lenders get paid first. Risk of total loss is balanced by the potential for greater reward in the form of price appreciation.

Company growth tends to be reflected in a rising share price, offering the potential for a gain on the capital you invested in addition to the dividend yield. These two components—dividends and gains—make up the "total return" potential of your invested capital. Importantly, stocks tend to be much more volatile than bonds in terms of price.

The Wall Street *brokerages* buy, sell, hold and trade securities (including stocks and bonds) for their customers' accounts. Wall Street *dealers* also own stock and bond inventories to facilitate customer transactions and earn proprietary trading returns. Broker/dealers do both. The money center commercial banks, like Bank of America, have wealth management arms that are their broker/dealer affiliates, like Merrill Lynch.

Like the global economy, the investment business too is always evolving. Traditional stock brokers can execute customer orders or make recommendations considered suitable based on their knowledge of the client's risk tolerance, investment objectives and time horizon. Fee-based portfolio managers at mutual fund companies, money management firms, and hedge funds usually require a free hand to buy and sell securities on a client's behalf, so handing over discretion to the portfolio manager is often mandatory. Commission-based brokers at the big bank "wire houses" and other execution-based brokerage firms typically require a client's consent to a trade before its execution.

Trading for Trading's Sake

With or without discretion and whether commission- or fee-based, the buying and selling of securities encapsulates the *raison d'être* of the Wall Street shadow banks, and securities trading is their lifeblood. But trading for trading's sake tends to invite speculation and receives criticism from buy-and-hold investors who tend to be more analytical and systematic.

Beginning in the late 1990s, stockbrokers took on the title "financial advisor" when the big wire houses shifted from a commission- to a fee-based revenue model and wanted to exude a more knowledgeable, caring and comprehensive approach to customer service. Fees are a steady income source that levels out brokerage-firm cash flow, so most firms prefer them to the less consistent flow derived from broker commissions.

Trading is a win/lose proposition that pits buyers and sellers against each other, with both sides seeking an advantage. Buyers want to spend less and sellers want to get more for their securities. Traditionally, investment securities are valued—or priced—based on specific free-market fundamentals. For bonds, the key metric is "yield," or the cash flow they generate. Yield translates into price: the lower the yield an investor is willing to accept, the higher the price that investor is willing to pay for a bond—the standard of "fixed income" investments.

Bonds reflect the forces of supply and demand in capital markets. If borrowing demand is high and money supply is low, the cost of money naturally rises and borrowers offer higher yields in the form of interest on the debt they issue. If money supply is plentiful and loan demand soft, lenders are likely to accept a lower rate for putting their surplus cash to work. In a free market, the forces of supply and demand naturally find equilibrium.

The ten-year US Treasury note (UST10Year) serves as the risk-free interest-rate benchmark on which all other public or private fixed-income instruments in the world are priced. This is a privilege afforded by the global US dollar-based currency reserve system initiated by the Bretton Woods Agreement of 1944. It means that by setting the interest rate on the UST10Year, the Federal Reserve can determine rates paid around the world on all manner of debt obligations. And, indirectly, influence stock prices as well.

Stocks are open-ended in terms of duration; they don't have a maturity date. Their key yield metrics come in the form of earnings and dividends. Historically, large-cap US companies are priced at an average 16 times their earnings (16x); i.e., if a company earned $5, its share price would be $90 on average. Of course, price-to-earnings (P/E) ratios vary over time, from as low as 5x to as high as 35x or more, based on market sentiment (herding), investor risk-appetite (on the fear-greed continuum), momentum (recency bias) or a host of other fundamental and psychological factors.

If they are selling at 5x, stock prices are historically underpriced and can be expected to trend higher; at 30x they are historically over-priced and could drop a lot lower. In a free market, the process is ineluctable. Market historians have shown that over long enough periods, stock prices always revert to their long-term average, their mean value, of 16x. If they start high above the mean they tend to overshoot to the downside; if they start far below the mean they tend to overshoot to the upside. But a return to the mean is inevitable.

In pricing a stock, complications can arise when "earnings" are quantified and their quality enters the equation. Earnings, as we have seen, can be manipulated. Are a company's reported earnings understated or overstated? Are they sustainable or do they reflect extraordinary one-time events that may not be replicable? Have sales been booked prematurely to magnify quarterly results or delayed to smooth earnings over several quarters? Certified Financial Analysts (CFA) are trained to focus on the fine print when evaluating a company's financial condition and business prospects to determine a fair price for its shares.

As defined by Benjamin Graham and David Dodd in their 1934 classic "Security Analysis," investing should be an informed, highly technical and exacting process practiced by trained professionals who seek to discover the intrinsic value of a business enterprise, buy its shares when the market price is below it, hold them until they reach full value, and then sell to reap a positive return. Renowned investors Warren Buffett and his partner Charlie Munger are said to be practitioners of this highly analytic and disciplined "value" approach to the process.

It is certainly plausible to think that professional investors operate this way. But it's a lot to ask of individuals, i.e., retail investors, who (let's admit) tend to follow the crowd and demonstrate insufficient investment discipline, especially when confronted by challenging circumstances. Undisciplined buying and selling in blind pursuit of returns more accurately qualifies as "speculation." The return shortfall suffered by average investors (who follow their instincts when they buy and sell mutual funds) is quantified by the annual Dalbar study. The shortfall amounts to half the statistical returns earned by the underlying funds that Dalbar tracks. The widely recognized shortfall is largely owed to bad timing and an undisciplined, speculative, approach. Supporting Dalbar's findings, the JPMorgan Fact Book confirms that the "average investor" trails the raw returns for various key asset classes and combination portfolios. It's widely believed in the industry that a key reason for this lag is the emotion-driven, poorly timed decision making that defines the investor life cycle, i.e., buying high and selling low.

FIGURE 28. AVERAGE INVESTOR PERFORMANCE TRAILS THE KEY MARKET RETURNS

Source: J.P. Morgan Asset Management, (Top) Barclay's, FactSet, Standard & Poor's, (Bottom) Dalbar, Inc.
Indexes used are as follows: REITS, NAREIT Equity RE/IT Index, EAFE:MSCI EAFE, Oi WTI Index, Bonds: Barclays U.S.
Aggregate Ind, Homes: Median sale price of existing single-family homes, Gold: USD oz., Inflation: CPI, 60/40: A balanced
portfolio with 60% invested in S&P 500 index and 40% invested in high quality U.S. fixed income, represented by the
Barclays U.S. Aggregate Index. The portfolio is rebalanced annually. Average asset allocation investor return is based on an
analysis by Dalbar Inc., which utilizes the net of aggregate mutual fund sales, redemptions and exchanges each month as
a measure of investor behavior. Returns are annualized (and total return where applicable) and represent the 20-year
period ending 12/31/16 to math Dalbar's most recent analysis.
Guide to the Markets - U.S. Data are as of December 31, 2017.

J.P.Morgan
Asset Management

Investment portfolio composition was traditionally based on astute stock selection grounded in shadow banker skill, experience, and training. Portfolio management was an effort to outperform the market as a whole. Outperformance was measured in terms of "alpha," the annual return earned in excess of the broad market averages. "Active" management that produced outperformance was worth paying for if the net result left you with more.

Since 2008, active management has been falling out of favor, replaced by "passive" investment management via mutual- and ex-change-traded funds (ETFs) that merely replicate the broad market indices at very low cost. The S&P Indices Versus Active Scorecard (SPIVA) reveals that since the Global Financial Crisis over 90 percent of active managers charging fees of 1% to 1.5% have in fact lagged the broad indices. This includes most hedge fund managers who previously boasted extraordinary market-beating returns based on their unique skill, information and timing, and charged 20% or more on all gains in addition to a 2%-3% management fee. Online robo-investing sites that offer low-cost, algorithm-based portfolio design services are accelerating the trend toward low-cost index-hugging investing. Retirees focused on saving money are said to be attracted to this approach, giving little thought to the associated risks that may be magnified by ETF exposure in a rush to the exits.

Business is Booming

Over the years, the Wall Street shadow banks have benefitted from Federal Reserve actions. Practiced globally, Quantitative Easing flooded the system with $5 to $10 trillion, bid down the rates on US Government debt and drove down the cost of money. Based on current measures, consumer prices were scarcely affected. The inflation instead showed up primarily in the prices of financial assets, i.e., stocks and bonds.

While driving up the prices of financial securities, the Fed's cheap money drove down the yields on bank deposits and government debt, previously the domain of risk-averse savers, specifically, many of the retirees reading this book.

Quantitative Easing and the Zero Interest Rate Policy put an end to the idea of "living off the interest" on one's savings. As Mauricio painfully found, low yields can make spending principal unavoidable, almost no matter how much you start with. To be certain, Federal Reserve actions have turned innumerable retirement savers into anxious speculators.

What You Need to Understand

An important concept that retirement investors need to understand is that underlying Wall Street's advice is a narrative that can give rise to exaggerated expectations and a methodology that can ultimately cause your undoing. Rather than buttressing the retirement process, the conventional principles of diversified investing, applied to retirement portfolios, may actually reduce portfolio reliability. Investing in securities at the wrong times and under adverse conditions can increase the odds that you run out of money; if you do make poorly timed decisions, then protecting yourself and improving your probability of success require you to self-impose austerity from the moment you start spending down.

In other words, centering your retirement portfolio on Wall Street's securities-driven risk/return tradeoff may be a formula for an insecure retirement. Why? The answer is volatility.

At the heart of all investing is the risk of loss, and investors must be compensated for bearing that risk. Over time, stocks have proven to be the riskiest asset class and consequently, their returns have been the highest. With the goal of maximizing total return, Wall Street has historically earned its role as intermediary via its stock-selecting prowess and equity management skills. Possessing the most tantalizing investor returns, and lucrative for both shadow banks and advisors alike, stocks rule the Street. The financial media inundate retail investors with minute-to-minute updates on the condition of equity markets because they are the focus of the retail investment mindset—the stars of the Wall Street whirligig, where the real money can be made (and lost).

Because they're riskier than bonds, stocks have historically enjoyed a "premium" built into their return of about 5.4% over the risk-free rate, as Professor Jeremy J. Siegel writes in his financial classic "Stocks for the Long Run." And the Street never tires of reminding us that, dating back to 1928, stocks have compounded between 9.53% and 11.42%, as painstakingly calculated by finance professor Aswath Damodaran's regularly-updated NYU tracking study, which is based on data from the St. Louis Federal Reserve archive (FRED). The implication for your portfolio? If you want to earn that kind of return, you should load up on stocks.

Importantly, what's not sufficiently emphasized is that the long-term average return (9.53% for example) was never actually delivered in any year over the entire 90-year timeframe.

FIGURE 29. THE MARKET'S BELL CURVE

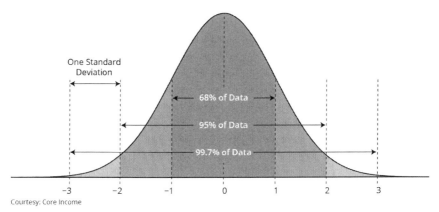

Courtesy: Core Income

Stock returns vary from year to year within a range (although sometimes outside the range), over what's called a normal statistical distribution, which takes the form of a bell curve. As illustrated in Figure 29, in a normal distribution, 70% of the time the actual return varies by 20% from the long-term average—a level of variance called

1 standard deviation (from the historical norm). If the long-term average stock return is 10%, then most of the time actual returns will range from a low of -10% to a high of +30%. Ninety-five percent of the time stock returns fall within two standard deviations, ranging from a low of -30% to a high of +50%. The remaining 5% of the time, what are called the "tails" at both ends of the curve, returns were even more extreme, consisting of market crashes (the S&P 500 index down 37% in 2008) and surges (tech stocks up 100% in 1999). Totally unpredictable, this variability is referred to as volatility. Year to year, stocks can be extremely volatile.

Over longer periods, stock markets have proven to be cyclical, experiencing multi-year periods when prices trend in one predominant direction, either rising or falling. These directional cycles are referred to as bull or bear markets. Since 1928, according to First Trust Portfolios, the average bull market has lasted 9.0 years, and the average bear market has lasted 1.4 years. Every business cycle has its accompanying bull or bear market, as recessions usually mean reduced profits and P/E ratios that result in lower stock prices, while booms produce higher corporate profits and greater investor willingness to pay a price based on a higher P/E ratio. Bull and bear markets follow each other because over time all markets revert to their mean (average) valuations. Reversion to the mean is a self-balancing internal dynamic that tempers market excess in either direction. Ultimately, as in all things, equilibrium is restored.

Although they comprise a much larger global market than stocks, bonds have delivered lower average returns that are tied closely to their actual yields. Since 1928, according to the NYU survey, the bellwether US 10-Year Treasury returned an average yield of 5.18%. Notably, bond returns have often been inversely correlated to those of stocks. When stocks have gone up in price, bonds have often gone down, and vice-versa. Although their returns have been quite competitive over certain periods (when they even outperformed equities), bonds are generally viewed on Wall Street as a source of portfolio stability and volatility reduction (with losses as high as 6% to 10% in any given year being extremely rare). Stocks, on the other hand, are thought to "power" return.

In a portfolio that includes both stocks and bonds, their inverse correlation is believed to moderate risk and smooth return over the long term, depending on the balance of the two asset classes. Combining stocks and bonds in a portfolio is called "diversification," and it's Wall Street's primary risk-management methodology.

FIGURE 30. DIVERSIFICATION BLENDS EQUITIES AND FIXED INCOME

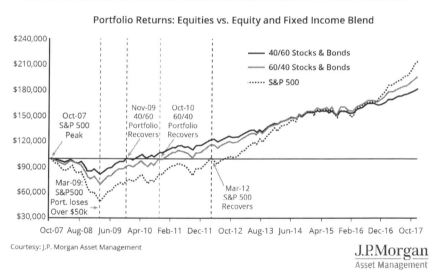

Courtesy: J.P. Morgan Asset Management

J.P.Morgan
Asset Management

The Wall Street Retirement Portfolio

The "balanced portfolio," which can sometimes over-weight stocks and at others over-weight bonds, has become Wall Street's signature retirement planning product. Applying Modern Portfolio Theory (MPT), it diversifies among stocks and bonds along an efficient frontier of return per unit of acceptable risk. A 60-40 stock/bond mix is deemed suitable by regulatory authorities for most individuals with median risk tolerance, so an advisor or firm can rarely be faulted for recommending it, even if an outcome falls into the rare extreme of return distribution. If the S&P 500 Index historically averages 10% growth per year and the UST 10-Year averages 5%, then a 60%/40% stock-bond portfolio can be expected to average 8% going forward, goes the oft-repeated incantation.

While the exact composition of each asset class may differ somewhat from firm to firm, most Wall Street customers end up with remarkably similar "investment policy" portfolios in terms of allocation, downside risk exposure and upside potential. Robo-advisors use algorithms built on the same assumptions to devise comparable ETF allocations. The whole process might be best described as a form of self-protective advisor herding. The homogeneity can be stunning and stultifying, but it's also considered reasonable and safe for all parties concerned.

However, the balanced portfolio can't always escape wide swings in value. Over eighteen months from its October 2007 peak to its March 2009 trough, a 60/40 stock-to-bond portfolio could easily have fallen by 40%. That's a heavy loss to tolerate in any portfolio, challenging many investors to stay invested, especially retirees who are tapping the portfolio for income. PIMCO Advisors cautions that the likelihood of "tail risk" events—i.e., extreme outcomes at both ends of a normal distribution (such as the aforementioned 40% drop in a 60/40 policy portfolio's value)—is heightened today, and that a fatter left tail implies a higher probability of extreme losses than the normal distribution would imply (Figure 31). PIMCO recommends that investors prepare by building protection into their portfolios, but recognizes that it's impossible to predict when a tail event might occur, making it impossible to time that protection. The logical deduction is that investors need a form of protection that can be in place at all times without costing so much that it devours their return in the process.

FIGURE 31. DEFINING FAT TAIL RISKS

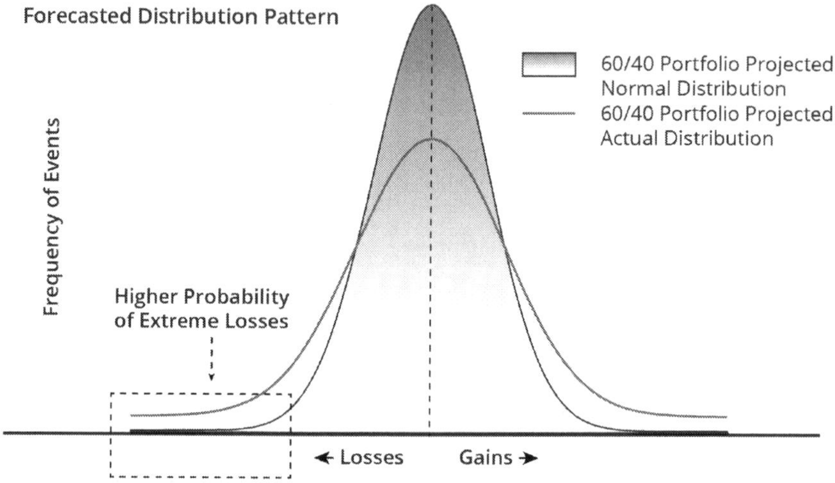

Source: PIMCO. For illustrative purposes only. In this distribution curve, the most probable returns, concentrated in the bulge near the center, have dropped, indicating returns likely to be more widely dispersed than those predicted by traditional curve.

Protection from unbearable losses can keep you invested, and the wisdom and practical imperative of staying invested through painful market declines—rather than trading in and out in an attempt to time the market's vicissitudes—is one of the most revered dicta on Wall Street. The historical record backs it up—given enough time, markets recover. Stepping to the sidelines at or near a market bottom often means sitting out a restorative recovery. Missing that snapback after selling low leaves investors to buy back in when the market has run higher. It's precisely this type of "average investor" behavior (buying high and selling low) that the Dalbar study tracks.

Only by staying invested through bull and bear markets—as hard as that may be for most of us—can we capture those elusive long-term market returns. Buying high and selling low renders those averages moot. That's why keeping you invested when your instinct is to flee may be your advisor's key added value, since you can assemble and occasionally rebalance an index-tracking 60/40 portfolio on your own using cheap ETFs. Resisting your self-preservative instinct to flee danger, however, is another matter.

Beware Exaggerated Expectations

Long-term index averages are also overstated for other reasons as well. First, as you're cautioned repeatedly, you cannot invest directly in an index. Indices are statistical averages calculated to track the aggregate performance of specific reference securities. The bellwether S&P 500 Index, for example, tracks the performance of the 500 largest US companies weighted by market capitalization, and representing 80% of the value of the 5,000 companies that are publicly traded. In a mechanical process that requires minimal skill, intermediaries assemble mutual funds or ETFs by buying and rebalancing the underlying shares that make up the index; the fund or ETF then mimics the index, and you can invest in one of those, for a fee. Fund and ETF companies compete savagely for your investment dollar by compressing the price you pay to blindly hug the index. Whether 25, 50 or 100 basis points (bps), your average performance will be reduced to reflect those fees. Despite the inherent contradiction implied, the loudest and most insistent retiree "investment advice" proffered by Wall Street today is to pay as little as possible for an intermediary's services. This is because, since 2008 at least, stock investing based on broad index averages has been effectively rendered skill-free.

Then there are taxes, including the stealth tax of inflation; the ever-rising cost of living that erodes the nominal value of your returns. Unless your investment portfolio is held in a tax-deferred vehicle like an IRA, 401(k), deferred annuity or life insurance policy, your annual earnings will be taxed as either ordinary income or capital gains. Inflation, averaging 2.88% over the past thirty years according to the Bureau of Labor Statistics, can never be deferred. In its most recent study of twenty-year market returns (1984-2015), Thornburg Investment Management calculated the real "real" return of the S&P 500 over the preceding thirty years at closer to 6%, or 40% less than the long-term average calculated from 1928, as follows:

TABLE 3. REAL "REAL" RETURN

1/1/1984 - 12/31/14	
Nominal Return	11.34
Fees & Expenses	0.55
Dividend Taxes	0.90
Capital Gains Taxes	0.63
Inflation	2.88
Real (real) Return	6.38

Source: Thornburg Investment Management

This result assumes the investor deposited a lump sum at inception and held the index fund through both peaks and valleys, making no additions or withdrawals. If we factor in Dalbar's behavioral drag of 50% (the cost of buying high and selling low), the "actual" real/"real" return may be closer to 3%!

Perhaps the most misleading aspect of the 8% average portfolio return myth is that it ignores the impact of timing. Investor returns depend on when in the market cycle an investment is made: Are you buying when prices are high and likely to fall or when they are low and more likely to rise? Your actual returns will also depend on how quickly after a correction or crash the market recovers: You have a life expectancy of 20-30 years at retirement—not 100—and can't wait too long for the market to get you back to the long-term average.

Above all, it is vital to keep in mind that those long-term averages are made up of returns that range widely over different periods. Consider these values assembled by the author from research done by the McKinsey Global Institute, Laurence B. Siegel, John Hussman and Allianz Global Investors.

TABLE 4. AVERAGE ANNUAL INFLATION-ADJUSTED TOTAL RETURNS

						Projected	
	1926-2016	1955-1981	1985-1999	2000-2009	2009-2017	2018-2029	2017-2036
S&P 500	5.9%	5.41%	15.22%	-3.50%	15%	0%	4%
US10-Yr	1.7%	-0.10%	6.56	5.08	2.0%	2.0%	0%
Period	Long Term	Financial Repression	Financial Boom	Financial Bust	Quant Easing	Shiller Cape	MGI Low

Sources: 1926 - 2016 McKinsey Global Institute (MGI), 1955 - 1981 Allianz Global Investors, 1985 - 1999 Laurence B. Siegel, PhD, 2000 - 2009 Aswath Damodaran/NYU, 2009 - 2017 Aswath Damodaran/NYU, 2017 - 2029 John Hussman PhD, 2017 - 2036 McKinsey Global Institute (MGI)

As shown in Table 4, the long-term average real return (i.e., net of inflation) is made up of a wide range of values reflecting different market cycles, economic conditions, and demographic trends. Though it is true that over the last 90 years stocks have delivered average nominal returns around 10% and bonds 5%, Allianz Global Investors reminds us that the last era of financial repression (from 1955 to 1981) saw 26 years of negative bond returns and only median stock returns. A 60/40 portfolio during that timeframe would have delivered a "real" return of barely 3% each year, nowhere near the 7% or 8% expected by pension fund managers and Wall Street advisors.

During the debt-driven "boom" that immediately followed (from 1982-1999), stocks enjoyed their longest run-up in history, averaging over 15% growth per year, while bonds also appreciated, due to the steep drop in UST 10-year interest rates from 14% in 1981 to around 6% in 1999. This rare, simultaneous bull market in both stocks and bonds coincided with the emergence of the baby boomers as investors. Millions started entering the market in the mid-1980s, driving up demand for financial assets while responding with irrational exuberance to the emergence of computer technology and the Internet. (Most boomers still remember this extraordinary period and like to think it's how investment markets work, feeding into their dangerously overconfident normalcy bias. They prefer to forget the decade that followed to avoid reliving the pain of their losses).

When the dotcom bubble burst, driving the technology-weighted NASDAQ index down 78% in 30 months (from 5,046 in March 2000 to 1,114 in October 2002), the totally unanticipated event triggered the first of two 50% crashes of the broader S&P 500 Index over the following eight years. Those crashes caught by total surprise the Wall Street analysts, economists and pundits who were confidently forecasting 12% annual returns for the unfolding digital age. As a result, investors who retired on January 1, 2000 endured a worst-possible scenario consisting of a 10-year period of negative equity returns, qualifying it as a lost decade and undermining whatever "plan" they might have devised that counted on equity markets to deliver their long-term "average" results.

The decade since 2008 is noteworthy for its outsized equity results. They're consistent with the Fed's asset pricing model and its intent to generate a wealth effect to stimulate consumption and investment. By lowering interest rates to near zero, the Fed increased the value of existing bonds by raising their currently offered prices to match the yield on new issues.

But the risk-free rate also sets expectations for stock dividends. The lower the acceptable dividend yield, the higher the acceptable price of a stock. By controlling rates, the Federal Reserve has shown that it can drive all asset prices to nosebleed-inducing valuations. At this writing, the S&P 500 Index, which offers an average dividend yield of 2%, is at an all-time high of over 2,500, having increased 250% since bottoming out at 666 in March 2009. Meanwhile, government bonds are expensive, yielding minimal interest just over 2%, fostering a preference for equity and equity's additional capital gain potential.

These factors cause worry among market historians and technicians relative to the direction of impending market returns.

The forecast returns shown in Table 4 were released in 2016 by the McKinsey Global Institute (MGI), the research arm of the renowned global consulting firm. In grim news for retirees described as "dangerously overconfident" about future market returns matching past experience, MGI predicts that over the next twenty years, asset class returns will fail to match those of the past 100, 50 or even 30 years, and fall short of the golden age many boomers remember and yearn for.

Basing its forecast on what it calls the fundamental economic and business "drivers of return" (GDP growth, productivity and profits among them) MGI forecasts a drop of 40% in global GDP over the next forty years, implying a slowing of GDP growth in the US to 1.9% over the next twenty. What are the causes? Similar to the symptoms of secular stagnation, they include an aging world where the number of working-age adults has stalled; a decline in wage and employment growth; a slowdown in population growth; and a stasis in technological innovation. Grounded in hard data, MGI advises retirees and their advisors to pare back the projections they've built into their plans and prepare to save more, retire later and *expect a lower standard of living once in retirement.*

Some noteworthy market historians forecast lower returns based on the "drivers of market action." John Hussman, PhD, CEO and Chief Investment Officer at Hussman Funds, is certainly one of the most respected. An accomplished mathematician with an encyclopedic knowledge of market history and an impressive track record as a market forecaster, Hussman argues that technical factors presage a sharp market reversion that is long overdue to complete the current market cycle dating back to 2009. While not the only valuation measure he uses, one of the most widely accepted metrics he applies is the Shiller CAPE, or cyclically adjusted price earnings ratio. The Shiller CAPE compares current share prices to inflation-adjusted earnings averaged over ten years, rather than to trailing or future single-year numbers. The latter can be manipulated for effect and tends to be volatile; elevated in a boom and depressed in a bust. Ten years is enough time for the economy to go in and out of recession, demonstrating how a company's earnings respond over a full business cycle.

The long-term median Shiller CAPE is 16x. As of this writing, it reads more than twice that, at 34x, and has reached this level only twice before, preceding the crashes of 1929 and 2000. This suggests that stocks are over-priced and may be heading toward a mean-reverting correction.

FIGURE 32. SHILLER CYCLICALLY ADJUSTED P/E RATIO (CAPE), 1880-2017

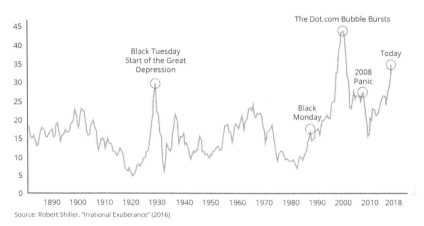

Source: Robert Shiller, "Irrational Exuberance" (2016)

Since its introduction, the CAPE ratio has proven an excellent predictor of ten-year forward stock returns. Looking ahead (as of mid-2017), Hussman calculates the expected 12-year S&P 500 return to be close to zero; his latest analysis pegs the 12-year prospective nominal total return of a 60/40 portfolio at about 1%, with bonds contributing virtually all of that return. Not alone among market observers, Hussman expects virtually no return from stocks during the next decade and also predicts a mean reversion that could be truly historic. Hussman's conclusions, though quite contrarian, have garnered minimal attention from the mainstream financial media — which is particularly disconcerting as equity markets continue to surge. While negative predictions are certainly not what we want to hear or believe, is it prudent to dismiss them as nothing but alarmist fear-mongering?

If a mean-reverting decade were to unfold, it could take numerous forms. Economist Harry Dent and others anticipate a sharp 1929-type stock crash that will plunge the market back to its historic mean, likely overshooting to the downside. Noted money manager John Grantham dreads a decade or more of low, grinding returns that will accomplish the same leveling, but over time. Either way, the next sequence of market returns could put the best Wall Street portfolio-based retirement plans in jeopardy of failure. Having to make sacrifices to accommodate market fluctuations, retirees invested in balanced portfolios may come to view this time and the coming decade as one of the worst in history to have been invested in stocks and bonds.

Say Goodbye to the 4% Rule

Focused on avoiding premature wealth depletion, the financial industry has gone to great lengths to adapt the "balanced Wall Street portfolio" to retirement planning. Starting in the early 1990s, its "thought-leaders" began over two decades of research to refine the portfolio's application to lifelong income generation, although this was never its intended purpose.

Originally designed as a diversified long-term wealth accumulation vehicle offering a tolerable level of risk, the balanced portfolio needed to be reconceived and reintroduced as a systematic income-generating vehicle similar to a pension or annuity. Retirement investors wanted to be confident that, just like a pension, their stock/bond/cash portfolios would pay out the income they needed without running out before they passed away.

Systematic decumulation for income was not the Wall Street financial advisor's bailiwick; it was the domain of pension managers and insurance companies. Maximizing wealth was Wall Street's value proposition. Advisors realized that research was needed to set acceptable parameters for an optimized implementation of the balanced securities portfolio. Optimization would give them confidence in the advice they offered, protect them from possible claims of malpractice and provide their clients with the needed product and service.

The first assumptions utilized for sustainable retirement income planning were the long-term averages for stocks (10%), bonds (5%) and inflation (3%). Assuming that they would consistently recur in the future, a 60/40 allocation was modeled to yield an average compounded nominal return of 8.2%. Since Wall Street financial advisors were not trained in actuarial science—and the variability of life expectancy overly complicated the calculations—advisors defaulted to a 30-year fixed duration to cover the great majority of retirees. Clients and advisors wanted to know what percentage of a starting balance could be withdrawn each year to provide the highest possible likelihood of generating the needed inflation-adjusted payouts for each of thirty years, at the end of which the fund would be exhausted. (The methodology made no provision for the 5%-10% of people who might live longer than thirty years after retirement; it also accepted a 10% "probability of failure" for portfolios depleted prematurely when faced with a "black hole" sequence of returns characterized by early losses).

Starting with these long-term averages it seemed logical that a 5% withdrawal rate would set a dependable floor. In 1994, recognizing that the long-term averages could not be relied upon because of the possibility of intervening financial disruptions (like stock market downturns and periods of high inflation), William Bengen, CFP[TM] published his benchmark study of actual historical returns from 1926 through 1976. Bengen's findings demonstrated that given a 50/50 stock-to-bond allocation, a 4% starting withdrawal rate would have succeeded for 90% of retirees even starting out in 1966. (That year turned out to be the worst to initiate retirement in the 20th Century because inflation rates took off while stock returns stayed relatively flat for the following decade). The "4% Rule" has set the floor for the "safe" maximum (safemax) withdrawal rate ever since. Bengen's research further showed that, based on the 20th Century historical record (and even factoring in a "black hole" scenario of sharp losses early in retirement), the recommended asset allocation was at least 50% stocks and preferably as high as 75%—a "testament to the enormous recovery power of the stock market," he explained.

FIGURE 33. BENGEN'S SAFEMAX 4% WITHDRAWAL RATE (1994)

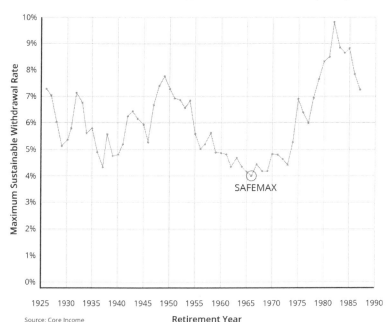

Source: Core Income   Retirement Year

Projecting future returns based on historical averages is known as "deterministic" modeling. It is a form of linear forecasting wherein expected returns do not vary over time—and that's its key flaw: the average return is most likely the one return an investor will *never* receive. Thanks to the increasing availability of computer power, "stochastic" modeling has grown in popularity. Applied to statistical sampling, stochastic modeling incorporates randomness. It has been tailored to retirement planning in the form of Monte Carlo simulations, named by one of its original developers after his favorite pastime—calculating the odds of winning at the casino.

In Monte Carlo computer software, returns and inflation are treated as random variables. Monte Carlo "engines" generate thousands, tens of thousands or even hundreds of thousands of possible combinations that produce a probability analysis, i.e., a statistical range of outcomes reflecting the financial impact of various return sequences. Now the standard retirement "modeling" tool, it perfectly captures the Wall Street approach to securities-based retirement planning by surrendering to uncertainty and accepting the necessity of playing the odds. The benefit of the Monte Carlo process is that it attempts to quantify those odds based on asset allocation and initial withdrawal rate. Its key limitation is that its output is determined by its users' inputs, i.e., the assumptions used for market returns, standard deviation, asset class correlations, inflation rates and numerous other statistical parameters. All projections generated are strictly hypothetical in nature based on assumptions that may prove inaccurate over time, do not reflect actual investment results and are not guarantees of future results. In fact, results may vary with each use and over time.

Changing the input assumptions and the type of mathematics used in a given Monte Carlo engine can materially alter the results. Critics focus on this subjectivity, which they claim introduces bias into the design. Mathematician and financial advisor James Otar, CFP[TM], argues that the methodology tends to overstate the probability of favorable outcomes, giving clients a dangerously exaggerated sense of security.

Leading researchers in retirement-income planning have recently published seminal studies that address these issues, with some surprising conclusions. Working together, professors Wade Pfau, PhD and Michael Finke, PhD, of the American College of Financial Planning, along with David Blanchett, CFA, CFP, head of retirement research at Morningstar Investment Management, tested the 4% Rule under historic return assumptions and then under forward-looking assumptions, illustrating the possibility of Shiller CAPE-based lower returns.

TABLE 5. RETURN ASSUMPTIONS: PAST VERSUS FUTURE

	(Nominal) Historical Returns	(Nominal) Forward Returns
S&P 500	12%	9%
US 10-Yr	5%	2.5%
CAPE Ratio	16	27

Source: Blanchett, Finke, & Pfau 2015

The group confirmed that based on historical data (stocks returning 12%, bonds returning 5% and a CAPE ratio of 16), a portfolio allocation to stocks of roughly 15% or more would have likely achieved a 90% probability or better that a portfolio would survive thirty years paying out 4% adjusted for inflation. But if future expectations are lowered based on current interest rates (bonds at 2.5%) and the reduced stock returns predicted by today's above-average CAPE ratio—even if lowered only modestly—the odds of success plummet, barely exceeding 50% no matter how high the stock allocation! This industry-standard Monte Carlo probability analysis conveys a stunning implication: Using forward-looking assumptions, Bengen's "the more stock the better" equity recommendation for portfolio reliability may be overstated. Given reduced future returns, it may even court disaster, driving the odds of 60/40 portfolio success down to 56%—or little better than a coin toss.

FIGURE 34. PROJECTED SUCCESS RATES

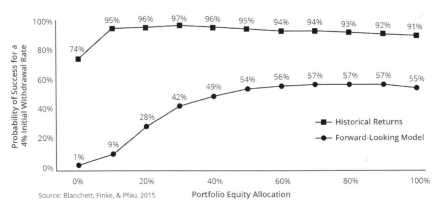

Source: Blanchett, Finke, & Pfau, 2015

Looking ahead based on lowered return expectations, Blanchett, Finke and Pfau questioned how a 90% (or higher) probability of portfolio success can be sustained. The answer: Only by *reducing* the withdrawal percentage in inverse ratio to the equity allocation; in other words, the *higher* the ratio of stock held in a portfolio, the *lower* the safe withdrawal rate you should use and the less income you should take.

TABLE 6. FORWARD-LOOKING SAFEMAX 30-YEAR WITHDRAWAL RATES

Equity Allocation	90% Probability	99% Probability
20%	3.1%	2.7%
40%	3.0	2.3
60%	2.8	1.9
80%	2.5	1.4

Source: Blanchett, Finke, & Pfau 2015

Two rather startling conclusions can be drawn from these findings. First, the more equity in your portfolio, the lower your safe withdrawal rate; second, the more near-certainty you crave, the lower your safe withdrawal rate must fall!

In light of market uncertainties ahead (rather than generating a wealth effect for you in retirement), over-weighting equity to 60%, for example, imposes austerity, limiting you to a floor of roughly 2.5% from the outset, rather than the previous standard of 4%. This means that to be prudent you should limit your withdrawals to about $25,000 on every $1 million in your nest egg.

Additionally, the more equity in your portfolio, the greater the potential tail risk to which it will be exposed. An extreme adverse market event (like a crash) endured during the first 5 to 10 years of retirement could raise the recovery hurdle beyond reach forever. Crashes don't usually happen to bonds (though they can) but you're signing up for them with stocks. The impact of a bad return sequence early on increases proportionately with your equity allocation because equity markets are inherently volatile.

Too little importance was previously attached to sequence of returns risk. This was the conclusion drawn by W. Van Harlow, PhD, CFA to explain his unexpected findings in a seminal 2011 study he oversaw as Director of Research for the Putnam Institute and Director of Retirement Investment Solutions for Putnam Investments. Having previously served as managing director of the Fidelity Research Institute and editor-in-chief of the Financial Analysts Journal, Van Harlow boasts professional credentials in math and financial economics that imbue his independent findings with unquestioned credibility. Beginning his research with the presumption that the 60/40 equity-to-fixed-income allocation would prove optimal, his conclusions shocked even him. By focusing his methodology on the "downside risk" to chart the most efficient allocation of asset classes for the greatest chance of avoiding a retirement plan failure, Van Harlow declared that the maximum allocation to stocks in a retirement portfolio should not exceed 5% to 25%, and that optimal stock allocations for 65-85-year-old individuals should be in the 5% to 10% range! When longevity and sequence of returns risks are properly factored in, he declared, it is critical to limit equity exposure and investment volatility to optimize the probability of avoiding retirement ruin.

This is not to say that bond markets *never* crash and that a 75% to 95% allocation to cash and bonds will therefore see you safely to your goal given today's low interest rates. Were interest rates to rise, a significant risk for retirees as one Fed Chair after another has talked up "normalization" to pre-GFC levels, bond values will fall as a multiple of their duration. A 1% rise in interest rates, for example, would cause a bond with a ten-year duration to drop 10% in price; a 2% rise would cause a 20% drop, and so on. According to the MGI study, a return to normalcy over the next ten years (i.e., a 5% return on the ten-year) could take the 10-year note to 10%, rising by approximately 1% per year. Were such a normalization to occur, the bonds in your portfolio would be losing value every year. Selling bonds into falling markets will require you to sell more of them to get the cash you need. It's a surefire way to go broke well before your retirement ends.

Retirees Should Plan for the Worst

The Fed's rate manipulations, coupled with the $68 trillion global government debt overhang, introduce an abnormally high level of risk to bond as well as stock prices. Further rate compression to accommodate financial repression will have unforeseeable consequences, potentially including years of negative real bond returns. Will a reversion to the mean crush stock prices and will secular stagnation cause a market recovery to last for decades as it has in Japan?

The tactic I recommend to withstand this perfect storm is the stable-core portfolio anchored to the FIA. The FIA can provide the stability of cash, access to the yield of investment-grade corporate bonds, and some of the growth potential of stocks—while sidestepping the downside market risks of both stocks *and* bonds.

But resetting your tactics first requires a mental reset. Until the early 1990s, retirement planning meant one thing: pension planning. A pension is a lifelong series of payments; if you were lucky enough to have one, you didn't care how your employer or fund manager allocated stocks, bonds and cash in the plan's underlying portfolio. All you cared about was the amount of the guaranteed cash flow you had coming and the certainty that it would last you—and your spouse—for your lifetimes. If asked the value of your pension, you gave an income number, just as you would today for your Social Security benefits.

Since when did you have to be a Wall Street maven making complex investment decisions confounded by all your behavioral biases to adequately provide for your retirement? Writing in the Harvard Business Review, Nobel Prize-winning Economist Robert C. Merton explains that the seminal shift in the retirement narrative occurred in the early 1990s, when what was once an add-on to traditional retirement planning—the 401(k)-defined contribution plan—replaced the defined benefit plan in corporate America. Playing directly into Wall Street's hands, the language of retirement was effectively reframed from income benefits to portfolio management.

The real "crisis" in retirement planning, Merton declares, is this fundamental shift in mindset that has proven itself to be detrimental. That's why it is critical to reorient your perception of the retirement planning landscape, see what your real objective should be, and then identify the tactics that will get you where you want to go.

According to Merton, it is time to turn the page on retirement planning once and for all. So go ahead. Turn the page.

Takeaways

1. Investing involves risk, including, in the worst case, a total and permanent loss of your principal. Past performance is no guarantee of future results. Neither asset allocation nor portfolio diversification guarantee profit or protect against loss in a declining market. Bonds are subject to interest rate risks. Bond prices generally fall when interest rates rise.

2. The projections or other information generated by Monte Carlo analysis tools regarding the likelihood of various investment outcomes are hypothetical in nature. They are based on assumptions that individuals provide, which could prove to be inaccurate over time. Probabilities do not reflect actual investment results and are by no means guarantees of future results. In fact, results may vary with each use and over time.

3. It is advisable to understand the risks, rules and ratios embedded in the financial dynamics of modern retirement if you want to avoid failure—regardless of how much money you have at the start.

4. Former Fed Chairman Ben Bernanke's "new normal" of very low interest rates has turned many yield-starved savers into return-chasing speculators.

5. Given current market valuations, the Shiller CAPE and other historical market metrics caution that equity returns over the next ten years or more may be lower than long-term averages might lead us to expect.

Questions for your financial advisor

1. Do you rely on a Monte Carlo "tool" to project the probability of my (our) retirement success, and does that mean you can manipulate its mathematical assumptions to reflect better or worse outcomes?

2. Do you counsel your clients to trust that the future is going to be rosy, or do you recommend they plan to withstand the worst while hoping for (and positioned to participate in) the best?

3. If I'm nearing or in retirement, what initial withdrawal percentage would you recommend to set a floor for distributions from my nest egg?

4. How did the balanced portfolio you're recommending perform peak to trough, i.e., from October 2007 to March 2009?

5. If we get a repeat of that performance at any time over the next ten years, what will it mean for my (our) withdrawals and standard of living thereafter?

Chapter 7

THE NON-BANKS

Not all nonbank financial institutions are included in

the International Monetary Fund definition of shadow banks.

In particular, insurance companies and pension funds are excluded.

Stanley Fischer, Former Federal Reserve Vice Chair
Frankfurt, Germany 2015

Large financial institutions in their own right, insurance companies are often lumped together with banks in people's minds, as if banks and insurance companies behave the same way when running their businesses, managing money or interacting with the financial system. Nothing could be further from the truth, and you need to understand the key differences when designing your portfolio. Working knowledge of the relevant distinctions in organization, purpose and function is essential to retirement portfolio construction, because it casts in clear relief the unique role played by insurers and insurance, contrasted against the role of Wall Street and securities in the retirement process.

That said, banks and insurance companies *do* share three important characteristics: both serve as financial intermediaries between savers and borrowers; both are big players in investment markets; and both have been subject to customer runs. Customer runs are demands for immediate liquidity in the form of cash money, although for good reasons insurers have had to deal with them with far less frequency.

Nevertheless, policyholder runs can happen. Even knowing that, though, I would never have expected it from Roger.

Roger's Run

Standing over six feet tall and exuding confidence in his erudition, Roger pioneered the post-WWII entry into Europe of what would become one of the world's largest management consulting firms. Cool and calculating when evaluating the best use of capital—his clients' or his own—Roger initiated me into the decision-shaping process he used in the C-Suite of massive global enterprises.

Roger and I were introduced in the late 1990s. As he reached the firm's official retirement age, I was assisting him in evaluating life insurance options for his personal estate-planning. Roger expected me to couch my recommendations in terms of a business school model that went through iteration after iteration based on changing assumptions. Policy design, underlying investment strategy and comparative advantage were all factors we explored, together with carrier commitment, balance sheet quality and agency ratings for financial strength and creditworthiness.

After an exhaustive survey of his options, Roger decided on a competitively-priced survivorship policy issued by a flagship carrier owned and operated in New York State by American International Group (AIG). At the time, AIG was the world's largest, fastest growing, and highest rated (AAA) insurance company, spearheaded by its hard-driving CEO Maurice Greenberg.

AIG was huge. Publicly-traded, it had a trillion-dollar balance sheet and 116,000 employees. One of the world's most admired companies, it integrated 70 US insurers and 175 non-US insurers doing business in 130 countries. In addition to its geographical diversification, its insurance offerings included both property and casualty as well as life and retirement services. Roger understood AIG's complexity and appreciated how its diverse exposures could enhance performance and offset risk. After all, though he was a management generalist, his specialty was the insurance sector!

You can imagine my surprise when he called in Autumn of 2008 after the US government announced the first installment of what would turn into a $182 billion bailout of AIG's holding company (the entity that managed its operating units), to tell me he wanted to surrender his policy. Roger was not the kind to panic. An experienced investor in hedge funds long before they became popular, he understood the complex trading strategies they used to extract gains from abstruse quantitative interrelationships, so he readily grasped how some of AIG's trading exposures brought it to the verge of insolvency.

And he also understood that the balance sheets of its life insurance subsidiaries were probably inviolate and likely held the reserves and surplus needed to meet policyholder obligations. I let him know that I had recently been notified to that effect by the New

York State Insurance Superintendent, who cautioned all NY State licensees not to "twist" AIG policies from client portfolios based on unsubstantiated rumors of reduced insurer claims-paying ability. The Superintendent made clear that he and the nation's other Insurance Commissioners were engaged in a non-stop review of AIG's subsidiaries and they were convinced that the company's life policies and annuities remained sound.

But as relevant as the quantitative metrics were, they did not carry the day. Roger wanted out and wrote a letter instructing me to proceed despite my repeated assurances regarding his AIG subsidiary's underlying financial strength. It turned out that Roger wasn't concerned about his insurer's current balance sheet. He was concerned about potential future surprises given the failure of the holding company's top executives to perform on the two key measures that, based on his decades of consulting experience, trumped all others: Enterprise Risk Management (ERM) and liquidity. Despite the exertions required and the fact that ten years had passed, Roger and his wife cashed in their policy and replaced their coverage.

AIG

AIG's high profile in the banking crisis ended up doing a tremendous disservice to the insurance industry by creating the impression that the insurance sector as a whole played a role in the systemic breakdown comparable to the one played by the big Wall Street investment banks. This was simply not the case, but it is important to understand the role the company did play to both need and justify its huge bailout. That's because I believe the insurance sector is indispensable to retirement planning and it is best practice not to paint the entire industry with a brush so broad that you deprive yourself of informed access to what could be an irreplaceable component of your retirement success.

In some ways, the recent financial crisis unfolded very differently from prior ones, though they all started from the same place, namely loans gone bad. The Great Depression was caused by a surge of risky lending in the 1920s, resulting in post-war European loan defaults and a tremendous number of unmet domestic margin calls, which led to the great market crash. Brought down by runs in the early 1930s, 40% of American banks—ten thousand mostly local ones—failed, leaving their depositors in ruin. In the 1980s, amid their most serious crisis since the 1930s, banks suffered big losses in commercial real estate and loans to developing countries. In his report to the International Conference on Bad Enterprise Debt, Loyola University Professor of Banking George Kaufman, PhD, explained that between 1980 and 1991, some 1,500 commercial and savings banks and 1,200 savings and loan associations (about 10% of all banks and 25% of all S&Ls at the beginning of the period) closed their doors. By comparison, no insurance company is known to have failed due to the Great Depression, and only a handful had to be resolved in the early 1990s when ensnared in the junk bond and commercial real estate collapse. Their policyholders were inconvenienced by having to wait for their guarantees to be met—but met they were—without government help in a process that illustrates exactly why insurers are permitted to make guarantees in the first place.

Thanks to unprecedented government intervention and taxpayer bailouts, the most recent lending crisis unfolded differently. It started from the same cause: bad loans, this time in the form of subprime residential mortgages. Since 1999, residential mortgage lending had begun to grow into an enormously profitable craze that inflated an unprecedented housing bubble. When non-performance and default of the subprime loans underpinning the bubble began to increase in 2006, the banks that held them faced liquidity and solvency problems that limited their lending to each other. Moreover, the impact of those bad loans was magnified by the "securitization" process that blended mortgages into pools backing synthetic securities that were then sold on to institutional investors, including other banks, insurance companies, portfolio managers, fund companies, endowments, hedge funds and pension managers. The crisis hit when the value of those complex mortgage-backed securities began to crumble.

No entities were more exposed to real estate in all its forms than Bear Stearns, Merrill Lynch and Lehman Brothers, the three major institutions that could not survive without changing form. To free up the other major banks invested in these securities that were paralyzing the financial system, the federal government authorized a $700 billion Toxic Asset Relief Program (TARP). TARP pumped $190 billion into the top ten US banks and another $55 billion into 582 others, purchasing the securities for cash and paying face value to take them off their books. Liquid again, the banks could theoretically get back to lending.

Other than AIG, only two insurance companies—The Hartford and Lincoln National—applied for and received TARP funds. To qualify for a relatively modest $4 billion combined, they first needed to call themselves banks, so they purchased thrifts. The companies needed cash to satisfy insurance regulators that the value of their statutory reserves (current assets plus the new capital) matched the value of their future liabilities, proving they were not insolvent and therefore in need of rehabilitation or, worse, conservatorship.

At the holding company level, AIG got itself into a unique set of difficulties that required it to beg for cash from the Federal Reserve and Treasury Department. In the Fall of 2008, the world's largest insurance company announced that it needed cash to satisfy derivatives contracts it had entered into with many of the world's largest banks. Cash payments were needed both to settle credit default swaps (sold by a London-based financial services unit of the company) as well as meet a collateral call triggered by the securities lending undertaken by some of AIG's US insurance subsidiaries.

The liquidity crunch was triggered by a collapse in the price of mortgage-backed securities. If the publicly-traded AIG were forced to sell its deep inventory at depressed valuations, it could spark its own bankruptcy and trigger a downward spiral in its stock price, as well as in the overall stock and bond markets. Heavily weighted in the S&P 500 Index and tracked by countless 401(k) accounts, its collapse would be felt personally by millions of investors. If it defaulted on its contracts, its 30 or so counterparties (including the world's leading commercial and investment banks), would suffer losses that might further destabilize them and, by viral contagion, disrupt world financial markets.

To management's ultimate chagrin, AIG's small but enormously profitable "Financial Products" unit (AIGFP) became the tiny tail that ended up wagging the giant dog. Set up as a bank, it fell under the oversight of the US Office of Thrift Supervision (OTS) and its Connecticut office was said to have housed a steady presence of OTS personnel.   Begun in 1987 by Joseph J. Cassano, a former executive with junk-bond dealer Drexel Burnham, AIGFP conducted its money-making operations out of London, the world money center notorious for lax oversight. Falling through the regulatory cracks, it conducted highly profitable non-insurance transactions involving aircraft leasing, consumer finance and, above all, derivatives trading.

Like cash, credit, stocks and bonds, derivatives are a set of financial instruments structured, underwritten, issued and traded by banks. According to the Office of the Controller of the Currency, only four of them—Goldman Sachs, JPMorgan Chase, Citigroup, and Bank of America—are believed to control over 90% of a market estimated to be worth over $1 quadrillion.

Derivatives are intricate financial contracts that derive their value from changes in the value of the underlying assets they track and to which they are said to "refer." Reference assets to which they can be linked include commodities, stocks, bonds, currencies, interest rates or market indices. Derivative contracts tend to be opaque: they include credit features, embedded interest charges and collateral arrangements that are not always obvious, and they stipulate specific conditions under which payments are to be made between the contracting parties.

Derivatives are also highly leveraged: at inception, relatively small, initial fees change hands between counterparties to initiate the transactions; thereafter, even small moves in the underlying reference security can cause a large difference in contract value. Because they require a relatively small initial outlay, derivatives are well suited to hedge and protect against downward price movements in the reference securities, or in the obverse, to speculate and bet on upward price gains.

Derivatives range in complexity (and cost) from "plain vanilla" options (puts and calls) and interest rate swaps (fixed rate for variable rate), to futures, forwards and more intricate credit-based contracts linked to securitized products. Although derided as "toxic" by Warren Buffett, not all derivatives deserve shunning. The plain vanilla variety, index call options, serves as the investment mechanism that captures return in the FIA and therefore plays a central role in the stable-core portfolio.

What caught AIG short were the more complex derivatives called Credit Default Swaps (CDS) that, since their introduction by JPMorgan in 1997, have become the most widely used type of credit derivative. According to as much history as can be pieced together, it was JPMorgan that suggested to AIGFP that it write these contracts on packages of debt known as "collateralized debt obligations" (CDOs). CDOs are composite securities linked to loan pools. In effect, AIGFP would be providing insurance to financial institutions holding CDOs in case the underlying loans defaulted or lost value. The huge profit potential it saw in this financial innovation prompted AIGFP to go all in, and for the next eight years it was paid billions in fees to cover potential losses in mortgage-backed and other securitized debt held by its American and European bank counterparties. Because the securities were rated Triple-A by virtue of their diversification, its risk models predicted that losses would rarely materialize and be negligible if they did.

As explained by Scott Harrington, Professor of Risk Management at the University of Pennsylvania's Wharton School of Finance, in effect AIGFP was insuring those securities against loss and getting paid what looked like premiums, in a practice that actually violated US insurance law and would never have been permitted by US or EU insurance regulators had it been discovered. That's because insurance law requires "insurable interest" and the provision of adequate insurer reserves to back up potential claims. Because AIG was so highly rated, the Financial Products subsidiary didn't have to post any collateral in the transactions, which made them even more profitable. And because the underlying instruments it was insuring were so highly rated, AIGFP didn't reserve anywhere near what would be needed to meet potential claims.

So, by year-end 2007, Harrington explains, AIGFP had $533 billion of credit default swaps outstanding, with $61 billion bearing some exposure to subprime mortgages, and very little in reserve when mortgage-backed securities started to decline in value. By the Fall of 2008, the credit agencies had proceeded with lowering the holding company's ratings. To meet the terms of its CDS contracts, AIG now had to post increasing amounts of collateral of its own to cover the losses its banking counterparties were hedged against, starting with about $20 billion in cash.

Adding to its duress, AIG had another problem linked to overexposure to mortgage-backed securities. Twelve of its life insurance subsidiaries (three regulated by the NY State Insurance Department) engaged in a "US securities lending program" which lent government and high-quality corporate bonds held in policyholder reserves to some of the biggest banks to help the banks meet their own liquidity and capital requirements. In addition to paying interest, the banks had to put up cash collateral. AIG invested almost all the cash it took in as collateral in a Triple-A securities pool, about 60% of which consisted of mortgage-backed securities, primarily residential (RMBS), to earn the enhanced return they were paying over equivalently-rated government bonds. When the credit agencies reduced AIG's rating in September 2008, the bank borrowers demanded the return of the cash they had put up to enter the transactions. Because of the illiquidity of the market at that moment for RMBS, AIG was unable to sell its holdings at anywhere near what it paid for them. Given the liquidity demands on the CDS portfolio, it didn't have the cash or marketable securities to meet its obligations without risking insolvency at the holding company level.

It was this financial bind, which had nothing to do with its subsidiaries' customary life, annuity and PC insurance functions, that brought the Federal Reserve and US Treasury into the picture. AIG needed $43 billion to return loan collateral it had received from its bank borrowers and $50 billion to cover MBS losses incurred by its bank counterparties. Between the Federal Reserve Bank of New York and the US Treasury TARP program, AIG received well over $123 billion to buy time for an orderly liquidation of its investment holdings and to sell off some of its subsidiaries. (It eventually did, and repaid its loans with interest—but not without downsizing and selling off valuable parts of itself. Humbled and reduced, AIG nevertheless remains in business).

Importantly, the first $123 billion received flowed directly to banks in the US and EU, in effect turning AIG into a conduit for funds flowing to its bank counterparties. It was *their* protection—and certainly not that of AIG's policyholders—that was a major purpose of the AIG bailout. Writing in The Nation, William Greider explained that "Bailing out AIG effectively meant rescuing Goldman Sachs, Morgan Stanley, Bank of America and Merrill Lynch (as well as dozens of European banks) from huge losses....in what turned into the biggest corporate bailout in history." Even after refusing to sacrifice by sharing the cost of their own recklessness, the banks were paid in full; not a haircut was taken. They ended up with 100 cents on every AIG dollar owed, thanks to the generosity of the American taxpayer who was called upon to pay their bill.

It was only through the highly leveraged activities of its offshore banking subsidiary that the insurance giant was painted into a liquidity corner.

And what if the government had not intervened and AIG had declared bankruptcy? In the September 2009 journal *Issue Analysis* Harrington described the company's derivatives trading: "AIG's CDS activities were not conducted by regulated insurance subsidiaries. Despite AIG's CDS problems, securities lending problems, exposure of other investments to mortgage defaults and its high leverage at the holding company level, *it is not clear that any of its insurance subsidiaries would have become insolvent if the government had decided not to intervene (emphasis added)*. At year-end 2008, AIG reported $35 billion of surplus under statutory accounting principles for its general insurance segment (P/C) and $25 billion for its life insurance and retirement services segment."

In other words, AIG's insurance subsidiaries had $60 billion *more* than what they needed to meet all policyholder obligations, even based on the statutory accounting practices used for evaluating an insurer's "legal reserves," which are far more conservative than Generally Accepted Accounting Principles (GAAP). These surpluses were what insurance regulators were pointing to when cautioning agents and brokers not to suggest that AIG's life and annuity policies were in danger.

Would a bankruptcy at the holding company level have motivated policyholders to surrender at the subsidiary level? Surely not if the nation's insurance commissioners, charged with protecting policy holder interests, had anything to say about it. But Roger, for one, insisted. He saw the CDS fiasco, operated out of London by a rogue unit that fell between the regulatory cracks, combined with the subsidiaries' excessive concentration in illiquid securities, to comprise a gross failure in enterprise risk management, his paramount measure of prospective long-term insurer performance. Roger did not start a trend, however. There was no run on AIG's insurance subsidiaries. At this writing, AIG remains a very big, global insurer. Its policyholders stuck.

Other Memorable Runs

Although rare, there *have* been some notorious runs on other insurers. According to Professor Harrington in his 1992 overview for the Cato Review of Business and Government, those companies that failed in the early 1990s faced debilitating liquidity demands in response to overexposure to asset classes that were plummeting in value. A stockholder-owned company, Executive Life, for example, held over 40% of its investment portfolio in junk bonds, the asset class that became its competitive calling card during the 1980s and that initially provided higher returns on its life, annuity and guaranteed investment contracts. When the high-yield bond market collapsed in the first half of 1990, the company's stock price plummeted, and policyholders lined up to surrender their policies for cash. The run at Executive Life was brutal: cash surrenders exceeded $3 billion in the year preceding its 1991 insolvency. The company failed.

The failure of Mutual Benefit Life that same year came as a big surprise. A mutual company founded in 1862 and owned by its policyholders, it historically enjoyed a conservative reputation but got caught up in the commercial real estate boom that toppled the S&Ls. As reported, the company invested $5 billion of its reserves in commercial mortgages with limited geographic diversification, 20% of which ended up in four projects that were classified as non-performing at the time of the company's demise. Mutual Benefit endured an estimated $1 billion in policyholder surrenders during the weeks leading up to its board's request for intervention by New Jersey regulators.

The collapse of junk bond and commercial real estate values reduced the value of the investment portfolios held by these insurers independent of any short-term liquidity pressure. Increased policyholder surrenders causing pressure to sell assets into down markets were the consequence rather than the cause of their problems, but they also worsened them. Both companies had to be disassembled, with parts sold off to others. Policyholders were given priority and were protected.

At the operating level, liquidity shortfalls, even if only temporary, have been the downfall of many deconstructed insurers. Even faced with brutal runs, however, historic insurance company failures that required complex regulatory resolution left policyholders whole, with contract guarantees intact. State insurance guarantee funds were sometimes tapped. Although possibly needing time to unwind, reserves were always there to be liquidated, topped up by surplus and capital. Perhaps most important, when it comes to the reputational damage that a failed guarantee would engender, it has become industry practice for healthy insurers to form "rescue parties." Under the direction of jurisdictional commissioners, these rescue parties encircle a wounded competitor and unburden it of both its assets and liabilities, while preserving all policyholders intact.

To date, meeting the bona fide commitments made by any one insurer has uniformly become the voluntary obligation of all insurance companies (who may otherwise be fiercely competitive), especially the industry leaders. This was the outcome for all those companies that failed in the 1980s and 1990s, and would more than likely have been the ultimate result had AIG and its subsidiary companies gone under.

Sadly, AIG's visibility left the impression that *insurance* was somehow a central component of the financial crisis, requiring the federal government to gear up its regulatory oversight, capital requirements and even licensing of insurance companies, especially those big enough to be considered systemically important. Leaving aside the morale risk and other unintended consequences that usually accompany federal regulation, the reality is that the insurance sector as a whole was largely on the periphery of the Global Financial Crisis—where it belonged—at least according to Professor Harrington.

Banks are Integral to the Financial System

The GFC was essentially a breakdown of the "financial system" and a case can be made that the "system" is comprised predominantly of the banks in their various permutations. If anything, the crisis exposed the credit-geared interconnectedness of banking institutions, the explosive leverage built into banking processes and the transmission of risk through shadow banking contagion.

Insurance companies participate in the financial system; they use it, but they are not integral to it. Were they to disappear, the financial system of borrowing and lending, buying and selling, saving and investing, and making and receiving payments would go on. (Though needless to say, other crucial economic needs of individuals, households and businesses would certainly go unmet).

While both banks and insurers are big players in investment markets (especially the long-term fixed income sector consisting of loans, mortgages, infrastructure assets and bonds), that's where the similarities end. They differ fundamentally in terms of their business models, balance sheets and investment methodologies, and those differences can be key to retirement portfolio design.

While creating money and managing the payment system are essential to banking, at its core banking is about facilitating leverage, the process of putting borrowed money to work. Carrying a cost, namely the interest paid to its owner, borrowed money naturally seeks to maximize its return; banks are known for being in the business of facilitating leverage for others. Putting relatively limited amounts of their own capital at risk (as little as possible), they borrow "deposits" from their customers and lend multiples of those deposits to economic actors—for a fee. The fractional reserve system enables the banks to increase their returns by lending the same deposit to ten or twenty borrowers depending on the "reserve requirements" (5% or 10%) set by the Fed and the presence or absence of credit-worthy borrowers.

While facilitating leverage for other sectors, it is also important to recognize that the banks themselves are highly leveraged institutions, carrying loans on their books that they have taken from, and made to, other banks. According to the Institute of International Finance, as of Q3 2017, global "financial sector" debt amounted to $58 trillion, having grown fourfold since 1997. Brought to light by the credit crisis of 2008, interbank lending is the lifeblood of the financial system. Their balance sheet exposure to one another serves as the linkage that interconnects the world's banks and sustains their operations; it's that same linkage that also transmits the shockwaves that can destabilize and render the entire system inoperable.

When Lehman Brothers was unable to find a lender for the funds it needed to meet its obligations—overnight—its inability to borrow caused not only its own collapse, but the paralysis of the entire international banking system!

Banks rely on this interdependent system to obtain liquidity when needed. Central banks around the world (that are connected to virtually all banks) demonstrate the degree to which banks can only function within an interdependent system. The trillions lent by the US and European central banks during the crisis attest to the systemic fragility of all the world's banks, their exposure to mutual contagion, and in the words of Christian Thimann, Professor of Risk Management at the Paris School of Economics, "their dependence on the center."

The world's central banks comprise an inter-connected dollar-dependent system, with the Federal Reserve at its core. According to a report from the Bank of International Settlements (BIS), after the Lehman collapse in October 2008, the world's central banks confronted a "dollar shortage" in their interbank funding that could have ballooned to as much as $6.5 trillion. Unbeknownst to most of us, the Federal Reserve leaped into the breach to keep the system from imploding. By December, the Fed issued $582 billion worth of Foreign Exchange (FX) liquidity "swaps" as a down payment to assure global lenders that it would provide whatever liquidity was necessary. Those swap lines effectively bailed out the entire world, making the Fed its global lender of last resort.

Figure 35 shows the complex systemic response that quietly preoccupied international bankers, as they worked to prevent fragility in one corner of the world from bringing down the entire temple. Clearly, money-center banking executives and the Federal Reserve governors and Open Market Committee Members had a considerable task in front of them.

FIGURE 35. BANKS ARE SYSTEMIC

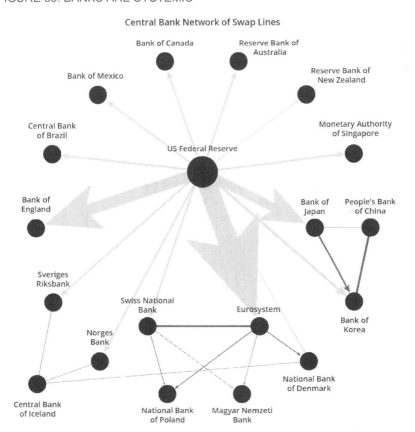

Central Bank Network of Swap Lines

Source: Central banks. The arrows indicate the direction of flows (where known); light shaded arrows represent US dollars provided to other central banks, dark arrows represent other currencies (evaluated at the average exchange rate during Q4 2008). The thickness of the arrows is proportional to the size of central bank swap lines, as announced; where swap lines are unlimited, the figure shows maximum usage instead, derived from auction allotments. The ASEAN swap network is not shown. Courtesy: zerohedge.com

Insurers are Peripheral

Compared to banks, insurers are much more parochial and inward looking. Insurers hedge people and property against risks in the form of natural disasters and death—hazards that can be fairly reliably predicted using statistical analysis and actuarial science. This has come to be colloquially referred to as the "law of large numbers." Insurers' social purpose is to protect policyholders from the losses they may incur due to the risks involved in meeting their long-term financial objectives; their economic purpose is to carry savings forward to meet long-term liabilities.

Here are some of the key ways insurers differ from banks:

Insurers absorb risk rather than transmit it.

Insurers are lone wolves. They're standalone operators, peripheral to the banking system, and don't band together to form a "system" of their own.

Insurers don't look to a central insurer for emergency liquidity.

Insurers don't lend to each other in the normal course of business, so they're not balance sheet-interconnected, and therefore bear little risk of mutual contagion.

Insurers shift risk from the individual to a pool of people similarly exposed and willing to share the cost of an adverse outcome by contributing a share of it in the form of a premium. In doing so, group members voluntarily agree to divide and conquer to keep damaged individuals financially whole.

Insurers manage the "risk pool," entering into contracts with the poolers that stipulate the conditions under which benefits will be paid, as well as the annual charge for the protection.

Life contracts are designed to hedge against the adverse economic consequences of two specific risks linked to life expectancy: dying before reaching it (mortality) and living beyond it (longevity).

Insurers are essentially long-term savings and hedging funds; their mandate is to accumulate long-term wealth and then systematically de-cumulate it over lengthy rundowns for groups of contract holders.

Asset Liability Matching (ALM)

Banking's Achilles heel is illiquidity in a crunch. Illiquidity can be stretched to the breaking point by a core banking process called "maturity transformation." An integral function of their business model, banks convert short-term liabilities—the deposits its customers can demand with little to no notice—into long-term assets, the loans it makes to its borrowers. Borrowing short and lending long can often lead to liquidity pressure, but it's this deliberate mismatch of assets to liabilities that generates the "spread" that earns banks their profits.

Conversely, the exact opposite is true for insurers. Insurers tend to be liquidity-rich, thanks to the regular inflows of premiums they receive. Insurers invest those premiums in high-grade liquid securities; they then set up roadblocks to deter policyholders from withdrawing funds early, by raising the specter of surrender charges and the possible loss of tax benefits.

An insurer's primary mandate is to match long-dated assets with long-dated liabilities (for example, a 30-year bond to a 30-year promise of income). Actuarial science can estimate the run-off of liabilities and assign probabilities to payouts, and insurance investment methodology starts from there. This process is known as asset-liability matching (ALM), and it aims specifically at timing cash flows from assets and maturities to meet projected cash flow requirements.

Like banks, insurers are large-scale investors in financial markets. Unlike banks, they neither lend nor borrow to make those investments. By contrast, borrowed funds flow through the banks and shadow banks of Wall Street, deployed to maximize their short-term returns, extract value from their trading advantages and capitalize on their preferred access to markets and information. Because borrowed funds bear an interest cost, they must be kept working—if not for productive uses then for speculative trading.

Borrowed funds (and leverage in general) have no place in an insurer's ALM investment methodology. Pursuing a liability-driven unleveraged investment approach, insurers invest to earn enough to meet projected liabilities. The premiums they receive are invested in portfolios of highly rated government and corporate bonds, mortgages, infrastructure assets, loans and (occasionally) equities. They are often held to maturity and carried on their books at par because of policyholder liquidity disincentives. Carrying savings forward in the form of policy reserves, insurers—in their role as intermediaries—are essentially deep-pocket investors that aren't pressured to trade in or out to avoid downturns or chase short-term results. Their time horizon is long, matching their clients' horizons. In the insurer's world, market downturns can become buying opportunities. Given their selectivity, prudence and buy-and-hold approach, insurers embody the best tenets of conservative Wall Street investment philosophy while employing their institutional strength and competitive advantages to the retirement process.

A True Innovation

Modern retirement planning starts with the recognition that—from beginning to end—it is riddled with financial risks. From market risk to longevity risk and a myriad of others that unfold as their byproducts, your nest egg needs to take them all into account to hedge, manage and minimize their impact. Modern retirement theory emphasizes that it's not the *return on* your assets that is key to portfolio design, but the successful *conversion of* your assets into a lifelong cash flow sufficient to meet your lifestyle goals—even in the face of erosive inflation and bad luck.

While banks commerce in risk, insurers are designed to protect against it. Banks make no promises. Insurers are only as good as the promises they keep. These two very different financial institutions comprise the two poles of the money management industry.

The stable-core retirement portfolio is built around an insurance contract that benefits from Asset Liability Matching and for the first time puts derivatives safely to work for average investors. It qualifies as a new asset class—neither a security nor a traditional insurance contract. To fully appreciate its groundbreaking potential, let's begin with a brief look at its principal precursors, the traditional fixed and variable annuities.

Takeaways

1. Banks are central to the financial system; insurers participate, but are peripheral.

2. Big bankers pride themselves on their global perspective and are sometimes described as "masters of the universe." Insurers (even big ones) are far lower key, and focus on meeting the financial guarantees they've made to their policyholders.

3. To meet those guarantees, insurers absorb and protect against many of the financial risks that bankers tend to propagate, such as equity market volatility and interest-rate uncertainty.

4. Insurers are cash rich and never borrow to leverage invested reserves to match their long-term obligations; a bank's profitability often rises and falls based on its leveraged gearing ratio.

5. Unlike banks, which trade, insurers tend to be buy-and-hold investors.

Questions for your financial advisor

1. Do you think insurers and insurance products have a place in retirement investing? If so, what might their role be?

2. Why do you think so many banks have failed in the past relative to so few insurers?

3. How do bankers and insurers go about their business, and what exactly differentiates their business models?

4. What is "ALM," and how does it differ from total-return investing?

5. How good do you think any insurance "guarantee" really is, and how can guarantees be credible if made decades in advance of coming due?

Chapter 8

POOLING GAINS

The value of risk pooling and mortality credits has acquired

the same scientific prestige and power as Newton's law of gravity.

You simply can't deny it.

Moshe A Milevsky, PhD, Professor of Finance
Chair, Schulich School of Business at York University

Life only, he insisted, and if it meant he'd have to come back from the dead to earn out, come back he would! Knowing Mayor Earl, his desire to be paid in full may have actually played a part in his miraculous recovery. Clinically dead for six minutes during open-heart surgery at the age of 83, this remarkable Southern gentleman—businessman, mayor, church deacon and *pater familias*—revived and went on to live four more years, counting his blessings, and raking in those guaranteed annuity payments.

A successful entrepreneur and magnanimous philanthropist, Earl knew how to give as well as get. We first met in 1993, when he visited New York City to execute the charitable and family trusts he painstakingly designed. A widower, Earl was focused on smart tax planning and benefitting his charities, while still preserving his hard-earned wealth for descendants.

Later that year, with everyone he cared about provided for, Earl felt finally free to focus on himself, and he had a very specific plan in mind. Earl had recently turned 70.5 and was now required by IRS rules to take at least the required minimum distributions from his rollover IRA. Instead, Earl decided that it made far more sense to turn it into guaranteed income for life by "annuitizing" it. Annuitizing meant maximizing instead of minimizing the payout each year without ever having to worry that the cash flow might run out. He was looking for the best deal he could get, and asked me to find it.

I did. Quotes from a dozen of the highest-rated annuity providers that summer averaged close to a 7% yield, but one stood out, offering closer to 8%. Even more surprising, it was Triple-A rated—ranked higher for creditworthiness and financial strength than some of the others that were big, but were rated lower and offered less! I recommended that we would certainly want to include that contract in a diversified portfolio of two or three contracts that would reduce the aggregate payout, but also diffuse any risk of default. But Earl wouldn't hear of it. He reminded me that you annuitize to maximize lifelong cash flow, and that was what he wanted. Earl wanted the maximum from his IRA starting immediately and lasting for as many years as he might live even if it were to age 100 or older—which was definitely his intention.

To fully maximize the payment stream, Earl was ready to take a "life only" term, meaning that if he were to die, his beneficiaries would forego any further payments. This was a bet he was willing to make, since he knew his children were already provided for from other sources. Earl postulated that if the payments were "guaranteed," why average them down? Earl insisted on committing the entire lump sum to that one Triple-A insurance company whose parent had been in operation for 123 years. Based in Canada, it also conducted business in Britain and the US. South of the border it held $8 billion in assets through its American subsidiary, Confederation Life and Annuity Company of Atlanta.

A year went by and Earl was happy receiving his monthly checks, knowing that the payout rate was the highest the market had to offer. And if Earl was happy, I was happy. But the happiness didn't last. A year later, in August 1994, the insurance world was shocked to learn that regulators in Canada had seized control of the parent company in the largest insurance company failure on record. Executive Life had been taken over by regulators in 1990 with $10 billion in assets; Mutual Benefit went down that year with $13 billion. Now, four years later and teetering on the brink of insolvency, Confederation Life was taken into receivership with a global asset total of $14 billion!

We soon learned that the company had been beset by big losses in its over-weighted real estate and mortgage portfolio. After concluding that its assets were no longer sufficient to adequately protect its policyholders and creditors, the board of directors voted to hand control of the company over to Canada's Superintendent of Financial Institutions.

With assets and liabilities spread across three nations, I suspected that this could get sticky. Even within the US, the company was based in Georgia, but its "port of entry" was Michigan, giving Michigan's insurance commissioner primary responsibility for putting the American branch into rehabilitation. Meanwhile, regulators from the Georgia Department of Insurance took control of Confederation's Atlanta-based American affiliate to oversee its administrative operations. The company had 18,000 US policyholders, but I was only worried about one of them. What if insurer rehabilitation meant an interruption in the flow or amount of Earl's monthly annuity payment? How long might this process drag on? Knowing Earl, I was sure he would be quite displeased by any disruption, especially one that entailed a failed "insurance guarantee." And if Earl was going to be unhappy, I was going to be unhappy.

In what is probably the most heavily regulated industry in the world, the insurance overseers from three national jurisdictions— focused on policyholder protection and fortunately speaking the same language—collaborated on a solution; industry majors showed up individually and in a consortium in both the US and Canada. By 1995, the US unit had been acquired by Pacific Life Insurance Co., which issued new contracts to Confederation's customers that promised the same benefits as their original contracts. During its relatively brief rehabilitation, payments to annuitants continued without abatement or interruption. Mayor Earl's cash flow didn't miss a beat. The guarantees held. Earl stayed happy, and so did I.

Caught in what could have proved a maelstrom, I learned that annuitants are treated as senior creditors when an insurance company gets into trouble. The goal is always to get them paid—in full—even before a company pays its rent. In a precedent-setting decision, the Canadian courts deemed that all of Confederation Life's trade creditors had to wait until after all policyholder obligations were met.

The Immediate Annuity

The insurance product that Mayor Earl bought exemplifies the "life annuity" in its purest form. A financial arrangement that predates stocks and bonds by thousands of years, an annuity is simply a stream of payments that one party promises to pay to another for a price. Since the 1750s, insurance companies have commercialized the process and have turned it into a science.

First and foremost a "life annuity" is a stream of income that simply cannot be outlived—it's longevity insurance. But if life insurers are in the business of designing, manufacturing and fulfilling the terms of life annuities, would it then be fair to say that life insurance companies exist to solve the primary retirement challenge of our day? Unlike the banking process, which generates retirement income as a side effect of securities trading and "wealth accum-ulation," scientific, open-ended retirement cash flow is the insurance sector's defining value-add, its specialty, its *raison d'être*.

Even more remarkably, annuitization not only guarantees a cash flow for life, it also maximizes the yield from every dollar of premium paid, and it does so at both the front and back ends of retirement.

The process starts with a lump sum paid to an insurance company in the form of a premium. The insurer then invests the premium to fund the installment payments it has promised. This involves carefully selecting liquid income-producing assets—mostly bonds—to generate the cash flows it will need to match its long-dated liabilities, while leaving enough to cover its operating expenses and profit.

Today, the investment process, policy design and pricing are all closely regulated. Under the terms of a straight life annuity, the payments are guaranteed to last an annuitant's lifetime, no matter how long. To manage life-long annuitization, an insurer must keep statistical records that enable it to reliably predict how long an average annuitant—male or female—can be expected to live. Calculating "average life expectancy" over a large pool of individuals is the work of actuaries. Life insurers employ actuarial science to forecast life expectancy for any individual of a given age and gender. In a large enough pool of such individuals, any one member may outlive his or her life expectancy, or die before reaching it. Mastering this "law of large numbers" allows insurers to manage the probabilities of life or death for a given age cohort. In doing so, actuarial science is harnessed to deliver economic value to the individual members of a given risk pool who choose not to assume that risk by themselves.

FIGURE 36. THREE SOURCES FUND AN INCOME ANNUITY

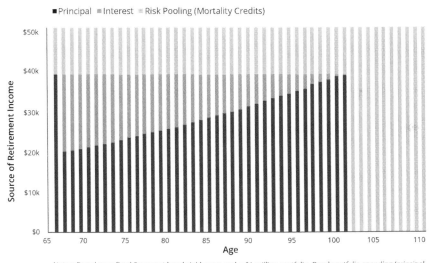

Notes: Based on a fixed 2 percent bond yield curve and a $1 million portfolio. Bond portfolio spending (principal, interest) is based on a planning age of 100. Annuity pricing is based on a life-only single female option using a 2 percent interest rate, Society of Actuaries 2012 Individual Annuity Mortality Tables (with improvements through 2016) and a 2 percent overhead charge.
Source: Retirement Researcher

A life annuity is a systematic spend-down of a lump sum over an individual's lifespan. For example, if we know that a male age 65 has a twenty-year average life expectancy, the insurer can pay the lump sum back to the annuitant at a rate of 5% per year, plus a share of the earnings generated by the premium while it's in the insurer's investment portfolio. In effect, the insured's premium becomes part of the insurer's general account assets. If an insurer earns 5% on its portfolio and needs 3% to pay for general and operating expenses, it can theoretically pay the insured the remaining 2%. Added to the 5% return of principal over twenty years, the earnings share takes the annual payout to 7% of the premium deposited. This is called the annuity "yield." The yield consists of both a systematic return of principal plus a share of annual gains generated by the premium paid. (The older the annuitant and the shorter their life expectancy, the faster the return of principal and the higher the effective yield, which is why immediate annuities get better with age).

An insurance company that can earn more on its portfolio while operating at a lower cost can enjoy a competitive advantage by paying more to its policyholders as it returns their principal. Confederation Life was paying more, but its underlying real estate investments stopped earning enough to support the promised yield, so management couldn't keep its commitments and the regulators took over. In today's ferociously competitive annuities market, insurers are constantly seeking to return more to their policyholders via innovative product design and/or enhanced investment selectivity.

Not surprisingly, the longevity guarantee must exact a price. Traditionally, a life annuitant who dies before reaching life expectancy is required to forfeit unused premiums to the pool. Quantified in advance by the actuaries, those unused premiums (left behind by annuitants who die early) fund the payments made to pool members who die later. The payments made to long-lived members of the pool—beyond the return of their premiums and share of earnings thereupon—are called "mortality credits." Mortality credits consist of other people's money (OPM); managing and distributing them is another unique value-add that insurers bring to the table.

Intensely supervised by all fifty states, the life insurance business model effectively permits insurers to shift wealth from one pool member to another based on mortality triggers. It's an ingenious economic device that assures survivors they will never run out of cash flow, even if they run out of their own savings and the earnings those savings can generate. Mortality credits reward annuitants for living long: By turning longevity from a threat of financial ruin into a promise of perpetuity, they transmute what could be a deprived *denouement* into a winning exit.

In this way, the insurance pool is composed of a community of individuals choosing to protect each other from the longevity risk they share. Applied to the needs and purposes of retirement planning, the pool maximizes cash flow from each member's capital contribution while alleviating the fear of depletion. At the outset, the systematic spend-down of principal adds heft to the yield, as the annuity pays principal and interest to the annuitant. Beyond life expectancy, the continuous harvest of mortality credits perpetuates and enhances the payout. Continuing the payout increases the rate of return on the premium paid. When it comes to retirement planning, therefore, the process of annuitization gives the insurance sector a tremendous edge over any asset management proposition.

Money managers may occasionally add alpha in the form of enhanced return to an investment portfolio, but they cannot add mortality credits, hence their portfolios always face depletion risk. Their sensible response is to impose austerity (belt-tightening) from the outset: Monte Carlo analysis has shown that in today's low-return environment, hedging longevity risk requires prudent withdrawals from a 50% stock/50% bond policy portfolio that begin between 2% to 3% of portfolio value. Consider how those "safemax" withdrawal rates compare to life annuity yields for males and females age 65 (even in today's low-return environment) that fall into the 6% to 7% range. It's twice the initial cash flow from each allocated dollar, doubling the marginal utility of every dollar you've accumulated in your retirement nest egg! In terms of generating lifelong income in today's low-bond return/high-risk equity environment, every annuitized dollar can do the work of two investment dollars.

It is important to remember that the economic purpose of the insurance sector is to shift and absorb risk to hedge individual client uncertainty and deliver predictable outcomes. So, whatever annuity yield is offered and for however long, the contract that binds insurer and annuitant is legally "guaranteed."

How are the guarantees met? Insurer reserves are their first backup. Fixed annuity premiums are comingled in an insurer's highly regulated general account that is invested in high quality assets chosen for safety, predictability, and liquidity. (An insurance company's rating reflects its general account's asset quality). Selected properly, insurer assets are matched to meet projected liabilities. Conceptualized simply it can be helpful to think of the portfolio as a collection of bond-paying coupons that are then paid out to policyholders. Both large and small insurers hold the majority of their assets in "productive" income-producing instruments.

Most noticeable, perhaps, is the near-absence of equities in most insurer general accounts, i.e., those stocks of publicly-traded corporations that can comprise 50% to 70% of a conventional "balanced" investment portfolio. This is because insurers eschew beta, or stock-driven market volatility. Beta is anathema in an insurance portfolio that holds assets guaranteed to match long-term liabilities. It's the source of adverse return sequence—a run of bad luck resulting in low or negative returns at the start of retirement—that can undermine the long-term reliability of any portfolio, especially one specifically tasked to meet long-dated withdrawal requirements. Minimizing beta helps reduce the second greatest threat to a retirement portfolio: return-sequence risk. In its role as a risk intermediary, the insurer's general account takes the place of an individual's managed portfolio. Stocks undermine predictability, and are therefore mostly absent from insurer portfolios.

While having mitigated sequence risk, the insurer's general account nevertheless remains threatened by credit and liquidity risks. Non-performing bonds or real estate can eat into expected investment returns, and we've seen how down markets confront insurers with unpalatable choices if they need to sell assets for quick cash. In an emergency, an insurer must look to its capital and surplus—usually 10% to 15% over its policy reserves. When insurer funds are deemed insufficient, the regulators are summoned to draw on state guarantee funds that protect annuity income and principal up to state-specific limits ($100K-$500K).

If the guarantee funds prove insufficient, the regulators swing into action to organize a rescue of the wobbly insurer by one or more of its stronger brethren. In the broadest sense, therefore, every *bona fide* insurer promise is backed by the industry as a whole, though this is not to suggest that getting caught in a relatively rare insurance failure couldn't be potentially disruptive, stressful and even costly. Carrier selection must be top of mind, and focused on avoiding regulatory entanglement.

Most Americans appreciate life annuities when they come in the form of pension and social security benefits. An employer pension taken as lifetime income is an immediate annuity that starts paying when you separate from service at retirement age. The guarantor may be the employer's pension fund backed up by the Pension Benefit Guarantee Corporation (PBGC) or an insurance company that accepts a lump sum equivalent as a premium from the employer and stands in the fund's place to guarantee the payout. The Social Security system annuitizes its benefits as well. Cardholders can't claim a lump sum, but must take income in the form of a life annuity that is guaranteed by the Federal Government, acting in the role of an insurance company, with its own actuarial tables, premium flows and trustees.

The Annuity Puzzle

So, the big question is, if the "guaranteed" commercial life annuity— one of the industry's signature products—can maximize initial yield, provide OPM when needed and eliminate depletion anxiety, why do so few people choose to buy it? According to its 2016 Review, the Insured Retirement Institute reports that the fixed life annuity currently represents around 5% of all annual annuity sales. Known to academics and advisors as the "annuity puzzle," the life annuity's relative lack of acceptance has been the subject of frustrated analysis for over half a century.

Why does the annuity anomaly persist? Steeped in behavioral finance, resistance to "letting go" is given as the most common reason. These feelings are not entirely unwarranted, as two of the income annuity's key features introduce psychological disincentives.

The first: giving up control over the premium paid. Once transferred to the insurer, the money becomes inaccessible, part of its reserves. Historically, and still with only few exceptions today, the income annuity is illiquid; you can't change your mind at a later time to recover what might remain of your original premium. Behavioral finance suggests that—framed as a "loss of control"—parting with money can bias an individual against commercial life annuities.

The second feature that carries drawbacks for retirees also relates to loss. While the lifetime income can be shared with a spouse, at death, whatever may remain of the original premium is pooled for the survivor cohort and not to heirs. Designed to maximize income from a given sum of capital, the immediate annuity is not *also* a legacy asset transferrable to descendants. For individuals with a "bequest motive," the life-only annuity may not be a suitable option.

For those individuals willing to "let go," the traditional life annuity suffers yet another significant shortcoming. While successfully hedging against both longevity and return sequence risks, it fails to address the third leg of the income stool: inflation risk. At 3% per year, inflation over twenty years will erode the purchasing power of your dollar by more than 50%, so the real value of a fixed annuity payout over the long term will be less than what it first appears. The question then, is, how to keep up with inflation without abandoning the other two essential legs of the stool? Is our only alternative a 50%+ allocation to stocks, which would require us to abandon the enhanced payout and back-end mortality credits of a guaranteed annuity, and potentially force us to live with self-imposed austerity in fear of depletion? Clearly, this is not an ideal tradeoff.

The challenge in keeping up with inflation is that it obviously costs money. Some life annuities are still available with built-in yearly cost-of-living adjustments (COLA) that increase payouts at either a fixed percentage or in tandem with a consumer price index (CPI). The drawback is that they can add 30% or more to the price of your cash flow, i.e., your premium will buy fewer dollars or you will pay considerably more to achieve your needed yield. Because of the added expense involved, inflation-adjusted life annuities are rarely purchased.

If desired, individuals *can* still find a life annuity that offers a variable payout designed to increase from year to year. Unlike the traditional life annuity Mayor Earl bought, a variable life annuity differs fundamentally in how its reserves are invested and its payout calculated. Rather than a portfolio of fixed income assets (primarily bonds and mortgages) that yields a predictable level payout stream, the variable immediate annuity is funded by a portfolio of equities held in a separate account. Like all equity-based portfolios, it fluctuates in value. Figure 37 illustrates that the variable immediate annuity is market-dependent and pays less some years and more in others. The payout structure doesn't guarantee consistent increases sufficient to keep up with a relentless rise in the cost of living. Instead, it's volatile. Depending on the market's return sequence, it can reduce your spendable income early in retirement and take years to climb back.

FIGURE 37. INSURED LIFETIME INCOME PATTERNS STARTING AT AGE 65

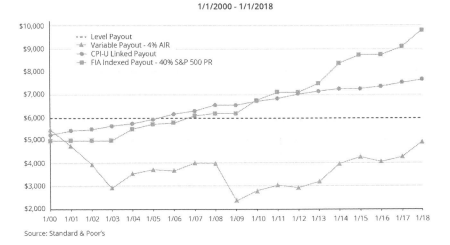

1/1/2000 - 1/1/2018

Source: Standard & Poor's

The Deferred Annuity

Given that immediate annuities make up such a small part of a trillion-dollar commercial annuity market, what are the annuities that *are* being sold, and how do they help retirees?

Making up the bulk of today's individual annuity market are "deferred annuities." Because they don't generate income from the outset, or ever, purists argue that "annuity" is actually a misnomer. While offering the option to annuitize, these instruments are really tax-deferred *accumulation* vehicles and statistics show that few of them ever turn on income.

Deferred annuities come in two types: fixed and variable.

In a "fixed" deferred annuity, premiums get deposited in the insurer's general account to compound (tax-deferred) until withdrawn or the policy is surrendered. The insurer guarantees both the rate of return and the payout.

The "variable" deferred annuity is a collection of stock and bond "sub-accounts" held by the insurer apart from its general account. This structure permits you to invest the same way you might in a securities brokerage account or mutual fund, but tax-deferred in the policy. As its name implies, a variable annuity's rate of return is not stable, but rather, varies with the stock, bond and money market funds chosen as investment options. Principal is not guaranteed, nor is there any certainty that you will earn any return on your investment. In fact, there is a risk that you will actually lose money. Unlike fixed contracts, variable annuities are securities registered with the Securities and Exchange Commission (SEC). The deferred variable annuity is also sometimes sweetened by the inclusion of added insurance guarantees. These can include a death benefit payable to beneficiaries at least equal to any initial premium paid (less withdrawals), just in case the annuity owner dies in a down market. The deferred variable annuity is most often cited for its hedge-fund-like management fees and expenses, which total about 3.5% per year on average.

Both fixed and variable deferred annuities require "letting go" during an initial surrender-charge period, and both usually include an option to annuitize, that according to findings released by Ruark Consulting, is triggered less than 5% of the time. If they were triggered, the income streams generated would still face purchasing power risk since they are either level by design or lock in once initiated (because the increased accumulation thresholds needed to grow them from year to year end up practically unreachable).

The GLWB Rider

Recognizing that letting go was the primary barrier to annuitization, in 2004 the insurance industry introduced a utilitarian alternative—a contractual "rider" referred to generically as the Guaranteed Lifetime Withdrawal Benefit (GLWB). This contractual addition committed the insurer to paying a guaranteed lifelong income, but gave the policy owner the right to access accumulation values before they were completely spent, and/or transfer to beneficiaries any remainder left unspent at time of death. The tradeoff is a reduced initial yield: At age 65, an individual payout may start at 4% to 5% of the policy's applicable balance rather than 6% to 7% paid by a traditional immediate life annuity. However, this is still more than today's prudent 2% to 3% return from a balanced securities portfolio.

The GLWB (Figure 38) is an actuarially calculated compromise that makes the ultimate triggering of the "withdrawal benefit" more palatable than irrevocable annuitization. Surviving beyond life expectancy will ultimately remove this asset from the estate, but only after it's been spent.

FIGURE 38. THE GLWB RIDER

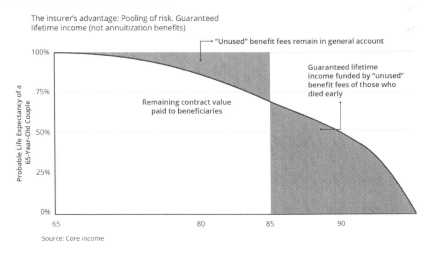

The insurer's advantage: Pooling of risk. Guaranteed lifetime income (not annuitization benefits)

"Unused" benefit fees remain in general account

Guaranteed lifetime income funded by "unused" benefit fees of those who died early

Remaining contract value paid to beneficiaries

Probable Life Expectancy of a 65-Year-Old Couple

Source: Core Income

Some Money Managers "Hate" Some Annuities

Destined to define the annuity category in the public's mind, the deferred variable burst onto the market in the 1980s. A hybrid financial product with recognizable insurance and investment features, it had to be registered as a security with the SEC. It appealed to both baby boomers beginning their careers as investors and financial conglomerates (the big banks and insurance companies) that were beginning to model themselves after supermarkets to offer a diverse menu of financial products in a "one-stop shop." Boomers started to visit their (appropriately licensed) bankers to buy life insurance and their (appropriately registered) insurance agents to buy mutual funds.

Amid this confusing amalgam of financial services, the relatively expensive deferred variable annuity gained rapid acceptance as a tax-deferred securities-based brokerage account-surrogate with added features that shifted some investment risk to the insurer. Risk-shifting could come in the form of a long-term guarantee of principal (the type that eventually got The Hartford into trouble after the 2008 market collapse) or as an income-benefit value that compounded independent of the investment account. Insulated from sequence risk, the income-benefit account could end up being worth more than the policy's investment account when called upon to fund a lifetime of guaranteed withdrawals.

By the mid-2000s, the deferred variable held a 70% share of the annuity market. During this time, it came to embody what the term "annuity" meant to most boomers—an expensive, complicated, high-commission and gated financial instrument with its own tax dynamics that wasn't always properly explained or understood when purchased.

In 1995, a product innovation quietly emerged that combined insurance and investment features in a new way that was not easy to categorize. Some say it verged on creating a new asset class, challenging conventional risk-return ratios and expectations. Educating investors about this product—the new annuity designed to anchor and not just complement your nest egg—is the purpose of this book. By advocating that it be central to portfolio construction and not merely incidental to it, I'm urging a complete shift in what may be your current *gestalt*, challenging you to transform background into foreground. I believe your retirement security may depend upon it.

Takeaways

1. Life annuities are financial instruments designed to produce maximum cash flow from a given sum of capital and are guaranteed contractually to last a lifetime—no matter how long.

2. Insurance companies have turned annuitization into a science that mitigates both longevity and return-sequence risks, which together, threaten premature portfolio depletion.

3. Relative to retirement income planning, the annuitization process gives the insurance sector a tremendous edge over any asset management proposition.

4. The annuity puzzle poses an important question: If commercial income annuities are so well designed to meet people's key retirement challenges (and so well accepted in the form of pension or social security benefits) how come so few individuals buy them?

5. The Guaranteed Lifetime Withdrawal Benefit (GLWB) rider was introduced to reduce resistance to elective annuitization by eliminating the need to permanently "let go" and "lose control" of the money invested while still guaranteed a lifelong income.

Questions for your financial advisor

1. Do you subscribe to a blanket condemnation of all annuities? If so, why?

2. What does the word "annuity" mean to you, and what feature(s) of annuities (if any) most put you off?

3. Are you trained and licensed to sell annuities?

4. If there is a particular type of annuity you favor, when do you use it and what do you consider its pros and cons?

5. Can you explain the differences between immediate and deferred annuities, both fixed and variable?

Chapter 9

IN A CLASS OF ITS OWN

The reality is at least some fixed index annuities

have produced returns that have been truly

competitive with certificates of deposit,

fixed rate annuities, taxable bond funds

and even equities at times.

David F. Babble, PhD, *Professor of Finance*
The Wharton School of Business, University of Pennsylvania

Simplicity was Wei's primary objective when she and her husband visited with me in 2005. I had noticed them, quietly attentive, sitting in the very back row of a crowded presentation one winter morning. I was gratified when I found that they were sufficiently motivated by something they heard to travel an hour to meet me the next day to share their remarkable story. As I would soon find out, theirs was a story that spanned the globe, embodied some of the most notable twists and turns of 20th Century history, and culminated with their realization of the American Dream.

Wei was born during World War II into a prominent Chinese family of physicians and property owners with deep roots in Shanghai. But when Mao Zedong's Communist forces took control in 1949, Wei's parents lost the family patrimony to government confiscation and decided that their daughter's future would be brighter if she left the mainland for Hong Kong, where relatives could take her in and get her an education. In Hong Kong, Wei worked hard and flourished, and within a few years ended up immigrating to the United States to attend college at Columbia University. While studying architecture, Wei met her future husband and business partner. Together, starting with very little, they set up a small company that designed lighting and other home furnishings for some of the leading architectural firms that were reshaping American commercial and residential design.

Hard working and soft spoken, the two built a thriving business and together created a lifestyle characterized by refined taste and efficient simplicity. While quietly proud of their material success, they never flaunted it or treated it as the purpose of their lives. They were artists. Yes, they were artists who capitalized on opportunities that presented themselves as they matured, and they lived tastefully. But they were always artists first.

By the time they came to my office, they had sold their company and were entering retirement. They were looking for an efficient investment approach that would protect and sustain them, without the burdens of anxiety, time-consuming administrative oversight, and the need to constantly attend to the markets' endless vagaries. They didn't want to spend their retirement years in service to their substantial nest egg, sitting at their broker's office watching the stock ticker, constantly on alert to make defensive changes to their portfolio on short notice. They wanted to design a nest egg that would serve *them*—safely, consistently, and predictably—while they went about their lives doing what they loved.

They were intrigued by the FIA's guarantees and securities-linked upside potential, but above all what was most attractive was its automated process. When it came to managing their retirement portfolio, they were seeking a low-maintenance user interface. And that's what really sold them – the potential to earn sufficient returns in an arrangement requiring no more than an annual review accompanied by some fine-tuning.

Their minds made up, Wei invested her IRA in an FIA that linked to the S&P 500 Index and credited indexed interest at the end of each policy year. Since opening the account, she has stayed the course, feeling no need to revisit it more than once a year on its anniversary. Despite the small sample – one person's track record with one FIA issued by one company at one point in time – after twelve years Wei's FIA has met her intended purpose. Her contract has given her returns she has judged to be quite satisfactory (without dropping in 2008 when the market crashed) and has given her access to those gains for her income needs. The result? Wei has been taking annual required minimum distributions (RMDs) and her policy value has grown, all without having to pay more than passing attention to the whole arrangement..

Complexity Under the Hood

While it offers the relative ease of "power steering," under its hood the FIA houses an admittedly complex engine that drives returns. Many retail investors have never seen one before, and are thus unaccustomed to its operations, leading regulators, consumer advocates and competitors to argue that the FIA's underlying structural complexity may be one of its primary drawbacks. The Fixed Index Annuity has received considerable criticism on this count, starting with the US Securities Exchange Commission (SEC), the Financial Industry Regulatory Association (FINRA) and the National Association of Insurance Commissioners (NAIC). All of these entities agree that the FIA is complex, and for that reason it is unusually difficult to even categorize. Is it a security that needs to be registered, or an insurance contract that doesn't? In the end, the FIA's insurance guarantees render it subject to NAIC supervision; its linkages to the stock markets require the SEC's input on how it's described; and the combination of the two leaves FINRA urging rigorous due diligence on the part of advisors before declaring that it's "right for you."

All of this commentary is fair. FINRA's 2005 "Complex Choice" alert cautions members of the public to "be prepared to ask your insurance agent, broker, financial planner or other financial professional lots of questions before deciding an FIA is right for you." This is sage advice, and one of the reasons this book includes over 50 of them. Let's address the complexity head on and see if we can cut through it enough to equip you (and your advisor) to properly evaluate the FIA's potential fit in your retirement portfolio.

At this writing, according to findings released by market-tracking firm Moore Market Intelligence, more than sixty-eight prominent American insurers have released over 400 FIAs since the first one (which was linked solely to the S&P 500 Price Index) was introduced in February 1995. Each FIA seeks to outperform in terms of excess interest credits, flexibility, predictability, and consistency. Each seeks competitive advantage by adding and/or tweaking its distinctive features. But like cars, all FIAs share the same chassis and drive train that distinguish them from all other investment vehicles, and it's those fundamental components that we need to understand to measure the FIA's unique potential contribution to a retirement asset mix.

Importantly, the fixed "index" annuity was not designed to compete directly with index investing nor to provide returns competitive with equity mutual funds or ETFs. Rather, it was designed for safety of principal and controlled volatility, with policy values enhanced by "excess" interest (linked to upside equity index performance) to out-return traditional rate-bound annuities. The FIA's characteristics of protection from market losses combined with market-linked upside potential reduce its correlation with stocks, bonds, and cash, earning it the privilege of being viewed by some as an asset class in its own right. Its standalone uniqueness is further underscored when deployed to anchor a "nest egg" that is tasked with generating lifelong retirement income: In the end, the FIA *is* an annuity, after all.

What's fundamentally different about the FIA? A **variable annuity** invests your values in stock and bond sub-accounts that capture market gains and suffer market losses directly. A **traditional annuity** earns a fixed rate of interest declared by an insurer based on its general account. A **fixed index annuity** is intended to generate higher potential policy returns without exposing accumulated policy capital to volatility and impairment. To accomplish this, derivatives are embedded in the product design. Derivatives serve as the FIA's "transmission." While many individual investors may view them as foreign, complex, or the province of professional traders (made up mostly of the bankers who run the market), a basic understanding of how they work is essential to appreciate the unique impetus they offer the retirement nest egg.

The "call" option is the basic derivative an insurance company uses to measure and credit gains in an FIA. Considered the most vanilla of options, a call is a contractual right to buy an asset at a specified price on a specified date in future. That right appreciates in value if the price of its reference security increases; otherwise, upon maturity, the right to buy expires with no value. Essentially, calls are contracts entered into by counterparties taking different sides of a trade, the buyer betting on a rising price, the seller betting on a lesser rise or decline. Upside-only options are used to capture value from a (rising) market without owning (and bearing the volatility of) the underlying securities. Insurers use the equity-driven appreciation in contract value to meet their obligations to policyholders based on the specific provisions stated in a given annuity policy. The obverse is also true: insurers quantify their obligations to policyholders based on the appreciation potential embedded in the options they buy.

But how do insurers fund their purchase of these upside-only calls? They buy them using a pre-determined "options budget" that comes from the underlying general-account interest that would otherwise be the amount you would earn in a traditional annuity. In the Fixed Index Annuity, you can choose to forego receiving this fixed rate, supplying your interest earnings to the insurance company instead.

Here's a hypothetical example: Let's say you put $100,000 into an FIA that earned you 2% (or $2,000) in annual fixed interest. If you instruct your insurer to use that $2,000 as an options budget that funds 100 one-year calls on the S&P 500 Index when the index is at

1000, and on the maturity date the index is at 1100, your insurer could theoretically buy the index from the option seller (its counterparty) for 1000 and sell it immediately for 1100 for a gain of $100 per contract—multiplied by 100 contracts held. At maturity, the 100 option contracts your insurer holds would be "in the money" to the tune of $10,000, and the insurer would theoretically credit your account with "excess interest" based on the FIA contract terms. In this example, a $10,000 credit would amount to 10% of your original $100,000 principal. In effect, your 2% interest credit will have earned you a 10% return on your accumulation value. In contrast, if the underlying index were to move against you, the $2,000 premium expended by the insurer on your behalf would be spent and the options held by the insurer would expire worthless, but your accumulated policy value would remain intact and you are free to try again with the following year's interest—if you are willing to risk earning nothing (again) for your efforts.

This is how the FIA ensures that your principal—the policy's accumulation value—is never directly exposed to market losses. The derivative purchased by your insurer enables you to participate in upside market potential, and at worst, expire worthless, limiting your maximum downside to the price paid for the option from the annual fixed interest you could have received. When index interest *is* earned, it is added to your policy accumulation value to compound. Once credited, index interest is never given back, so you never spend time recovering from down markets. Your worst-case scenario in any single year is a zero for your efforts. (Product enhancements over the last twenty years have been focused on minimizing the incidence of zero-gain years without sacrificing upside exposure in the process).

Let's Get Dirty

When an insurer buys calls it looks to the capital markets to find counterparties offering the most upside potential for the lowest price. Their counterparties are the biggest Wall Street banks that "make" the derivatives market, structuring contractual terms and setting prices. Pricing an index call option and tracking its changing value during the period leading up to its exercise is accomplished via the Black-Scholes Option Pricing Formula. Developed by Fisher Black, Myron Scholes and Robert Merton in the early 1970s, their Nobel-prize-winning pricing model is one of the 20th Century's most important advances in financial engineering. Prior to its development there was no standard way to price options, so, in a very real sense, the Black-Scholes model initiated the modern era of financial derivatives.

The option price is called a "premium" that you pay up front at the start of the contract. It remains to be negotiated how much this premium is going to end up paying off. Obviously, options sellers want to limit their potential losses and maximize their potential profits in making the sale.

The model assigns value to an equity option by weighing three factors: the volatility of the underlying index, the time left until the option expires, and the risk-free rate of return earned by the seller for the duration of the contract on the premium paid. Thus, if the underlying index is considered volatile, there is more potential for an option to change value and be worth something at maturity; the longer the investor may have to wait to exercise an option, the more uncertain that future value will be; while the higher the risk-free rate measured by the US Treasury 1-year yield, the higher the option's cost. The math can be very complicated in this area, hence the prevalence of PhD-type "quantitative analysts" running the business and their specialized computer programs enabling them to make rapid real-time calculations.

At the outset of a given crediting period, the insurer defines its policy-crediting obligations in the form of a crediting formula. Call options are designed explicitly for the FIA marketplace, constructed so that any counterparty payoff to an insurer matches precisely with the contractual obligation owed by the insurer to the policyholder.

Call options—and their mirror-image crediting formulas—can take varying forms. In order to assure a zero floor in the call option (i.e., to avoid all losses), an "upside" tradeoff must be embedded to limit the option seller's potential downside risk. The three key market factors that drive the Black-Scholes pricing model—volatility, time, and the risk-free rate—determine the bounds of a given formula. They are expressed in the FIA option structure as Participation (the percent of any gain in the underlying index that the annuity investor receives); Spread (a fee percentage subtracted from the potential profit before the investor's annuity contract is credited); and Cap (a cut-off level measured by a percentage of gain above which the option does not participate and the annuity no longer has the stock index's gain applied).

Insurers and the Wall Street banks negotiate option prices based on capital market conditions. When it does, the insurance company acts for the policyholder's account, deploying policy-owner funds and passing through returns. As we know, insurers are in the business of asset-liability matching, a buy-and-hold discipline designed to meet future policyholder obligations and guarantees. Up to very strict limits, NAIC regulation permits insurers to buy derivatives if they can demonstrate that they are solely to hedge specific portfolio risks, and even to sell them on assets they own to increase revenue, but the NAIC frowns upon the use of derivatives for purely speculative purposes.

The fact that, in principle, the insurer makes its money from a share of the coupon interest paid by the bonds in its general account puts a policyholder and issuer on the same side of the table when negotiating option prices with the banks. The insurer wants to get your option budget the best terms the market will allow per dollar of premium to maximize the potential earnings it will use to credit "excess interest" to your account. The more you earn, the more the insurer can boast about the consumer-friendly performance and proprietary policy design it offers. The more know-how and buying leverage it can bring to bear, the better the pricing your insurer should be able to deliver.

Insurers *do* have an indirect say about the caps, spreads and participation rates delimiting an interest-crediting formula when these provisions renew annually, however. This is because the insurer's share of its general account's yield gets paid first, including enough to cover all operating expenses and a profit. In a traditional annuity, it's the remainder that is paid to the policyholder in the form of "declared" interest. In the FIA, however, it's the declared interest (or the portion of it you designate) that comprises the options budget used to determine the degree of upside potential an insurer may negotiate.

In a given interest rate environment, the more paid for an option, the higher the participation rates and caps—and lower any spreads— should be. If insurer expenses rise and end up reducing the net available for the options budget, policy owners whose insurers have less to spend may wind up with lower upside potential in the form of lower participation rates, lower caps, and higher spreads. In the long run, therefore, issuer financial strength and expense management can play a meaningful role in policy performance, in addition to ever-changing capital markets pricing factors. Thus, insurer character reflected in its historic renewal rates is important to investors.

The Banks Limit Their Downside Risk

The call options designed by the banks to accommodate FIA providers can come in a myriad of shapes, sizes, and durations. Let's look at the three common structures used by most insurers to measure "excess interest." The interest attributes (participation, caps, and spreads) are applicable to any index to which you may link, and there has been a rapid proliferation of these indices since this concept was first introduced. Originally just the S&P 500, linkable indices now include the Nasdaq-100, the DJIA, the Russell 2000, the FTSE 100, and Barclay's US Aggregate Bond Index, among others. Aiming to control volatility, enhance return, maintain consistency, and limit price fluctuations, some very big banks and money management firms (including Barclay's, Goldman Sachs and PIMCO) have synthesized hybrids by applying proprietary algorithms to an active blend of some of the fundamental indices.

The amount of excess interest you can earn depends on the index you choose, the formula attributes conveyed by the insurance company, and the crediting method used to track the index. Today, three basic methods are commonly used to measure gain from one crediting period to the next: point-to-point with a cap and/or participation rate; point-to-point with a monthly cap; and monthly average with a spread.

One or more of these three measures can be applied to each index selected for any crediting period. Each will have its moment in the sun based on varying real-world market vicissitudes:

Often viewed as the simplest, the point-to-point method with a cap and/or participation rate uses the index value from only two points in time. On your contract's pre-set anniversary, the beginning index value is compared to the ending index value; the percentage of change is calculated; and if the ending index value is higher than the beginning index value, you will receive the indexed interest up to the declared cap or as defined by the participation rate. If the change is negative, your policy value will not be reduced by any losses. The count for the next crediting period then begins anew.

Using the monthly sum method, each month the index value is compared to the prior month's value and the percentage of change is calculated up to the declared monthly cap. At the end of the crediting period, the contract's capped monthly increases and uncapped decreases are added up. The net result, if positive, is paid as indexed interest; if negative, your policy value is not affected, and the count for the next year starts anew.

The monthly average calculation records the index values at the end of each month. At the end of the crediting period, those index values are added together and then divided by the number of months in the crediting period to determine the average value;

the starting index value is subtracted from the average value, and the result is divided by the starting index value to calculate the percentage gain or loss. If positive, the spread percentage is subtracted, and the net gain is then credited; if negative, you suffer no losses, and the count for the next year starts anew.

No one crediting method has proven to consistently deliver the greatest potential results. When the insurance company bids its options budget to its counterparties at any given point in time, prevailing capital market conditions determine the caps, participation rates, and spreads it gets at inception, effectively giving all three methodologies the same implied value at the outset. But as time unfolds, one crediting method often gets better results than the others, reflecting actual market dynamics during the specific crediting period:

The annual point-to-point crediting method can provide a measure of stability to counterbalance situations like mid-period index declines. With point-to-point crediting, a brief burst of poor per-formance may have a more modest effect on results.

The monthly average crediting method can provide a measure of stability in turbulent markets. Monthly average crediting has no cap on increases, so you can take advantage of large monthly rises in the index. It is important to keep in mind, however, that the indexed interest rate is reduced by an annual spread before it is credited.

The monthly sum crediting method can capture high gains in years that do not suffer sharp monthly drops in index performance; it offers significant interest potential in any given year, but results depend entirely on market dynamics.

As a general rule, when conservatively priced, a one-year options budget seeks to capture 40% of the price appreciation of the underlying index. In other words, it targets a 40% participation rate. So, if the S&P 500 Price Index is expected to generate a 10% return, a Fixed Index Annuity linked to it will seek to price its options to capture a return of 4%. If the S&P 500 returns 8%, a properly priced FIA linked to it seeks to return 3.2%. If the index returns an average of 12%, the FIA is designed to optimally capture 4.8%. Reflecting that 40% participation, conservative return expectations for 12-month FIA derivatives range somewhere between 3% to 5%.

This is not to say that in some years a FIA can't return more. Starting with the same options budget and implied value, more than twenty years of industry data illustrate the impact of unpredictable market dynamics on individual methodology results. They demonstrate that while in given years some methodologies significantly trail raw index performance—as would be expected—in others, a given methodology can earn the majority of an index's gains.

The Reset

The feature of the FIA that best underscores its potential utility for retirees today is the periodic "reset." After locking in any index credits, the FIA resets the clock and the new starting index value at the outset of each policy-crediting period. Thus, if markets crash during one crediting period, you may receive no interest but your opportunity to gain value starts anew for the coming period— *calculating gain from the low point you've reached.* In effect, you don't have to recover losses and reach former highs before you can further grow your capital. Market crashes therefore do not have the same negative impact on the FIA contract as they would with other investment products. In addition, when starting from a new low the likelihood of follow-on gains rises, because as history tells us, the harder markets fall, the stronger they bounce back. It's in the bounce back that gains in an FIA are stacked on top of preserved principal, mitigating the long-term impact of foregone return in some good years. Most individual investors miss out on these upside phases of market cycles and their compounding effects because they have sold in panic at or near the bottom.

FIGURE 39. THE HYPOTHETICAL ACCUMULATION PATH OF AN ANNUAL-RESET FIA CAPTURING 40% OF THE S&P 500 PRICE INDEX WHILE AVOIDING ALL LOSSES

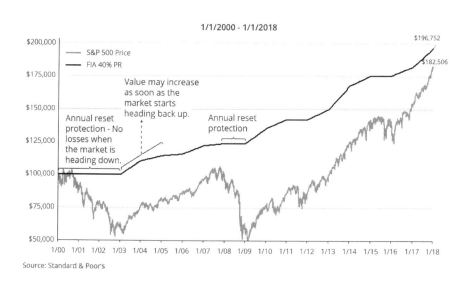

By significantly reducing the need for panic, the reset feature enables you to accumulate gains even in bear markets. Figure 39 illustrates the intended performance pattern of an "annual reset" FIA priced to capture 40% of the return generated by the S&P 500 Price Index over every calendar year since 2000. The example shows that while no gains may have been racked up in down years, no value was lost either. When gains *were* credited, they were compounded on the annuity's entire balance. As a result, the FIA provided a much smoother ride—helping you stay invested—and may still have met your wealth accumulation and retirement income objectives. That is its primary goal.

Migrating into the Mainstream

The FIA's performance features and its potential role as a key—if not predominant—component of a retirement portfolio may be on the verge of a mainstream boost, thanks to the research announced in early 2018 by Yale Professor Emeritus of Finance Roger G. Ibbotson, PhD. Professor Ibbotson's painstaking academic research over a long and storied career at Yale and as Chairman of Ibbotson Associates has informed the conventional wisdom offered to investors and retirees by the financial services industry, to wit: *Stocks have beaten bonds by a significant margin over time and are needed in a portfolio in order to generate long-term growth, but they are riskier than bonds, so as an investor approaches and/or enters retirement, it makes sense to de-risk the retirement portfolio by shifting its weighting toward bonds to reduce volatility.*

While Ibbotson and others in academia have long argued in favor of including annuities in retirement portfolios (at least since publication of the monograph he prepared with Milevsky, Chen and

Zhu in 2007 for the Research Foundation of CFA Institute entitled "Lifetime Financial Advice: Human Capital, Asset Allocation and Insurance"), his most recent research has focused on the FIA specifically, evaluating it as an asset class and portfolio component. Upon analysis of his findings, Professor Ibbotson has declared that Fixed Index Annuities can outperform bonds under certain circumstances, and should be considered a bond alternative in retirement portfolios.

TABLE 7. EVALUATING THE FIA AS AN ASSET CLASS IN ITS OWN RIGHT

FIA Hypothetical Net Return (1927-2016)

	Large Cap Stocks	Long Term Gov't Bonds	FIA
Annualized Return	9.92%	5.32%	5.81%
Standard Deviation	19.99%	9.97%	10.01%
Minimum Annualized 3-Year Return	-27.00%	-2.32%	0.00%
Maximum Annualized 3-Year Return	30.76%	23.30%	27.56%

Source: 2017 SBBI Yearbook, Roger G. Ibbotson, Duff & Phelps; Zebra Capital; AnnGen Development, LLC

Ibbotson is best known for his authoritative Stock, Bonds, Bills and Inflation (SBBI) chart that measures asset class performance since 1927. Using similar back-testing methodology, he and his team ran hypothetical return simulations from 1927 to 2016 and found that, net of fees, a Fixed Index Annuity linked to an uncapped S&P 500 Price Index with a three-year reset would have enjoyed an average 60% participation rate and earned an annualized return of 5.81%, out-performing long-term government bonds at 5.32%. In his 2018 white paper, "Fixed Index Annuities: Consider the Alternative," Ibbotson stressed that the competitive return was achieved without any downside risk, a fact especially relevant to him as long-term bond yields under 3% head higher in tandem with the Fed's impending rate-normalization process.

Ibbotson and his team also simulated various portfolios and how they would have performed in both low- and high-return bond environments. Note that according to his analysis, a 60% Stocks/40% Bonds portfolio underperformed a 60% Stocks/40% FIA portfolio when median bond returns were below average, a key concern for him in the decade(s) ahead.

In addition to the effect of rising rates on bond values, Ibbotson has also expressed concern that the stock market may be overvalued and heading for a correction. With so much risk over-hanging these two core asset classes, he argues that the FIA may offer a unique opportunity to "de-risk" without giving up at least a portion of equity returns. Thus, Ibbotson argues that in an otherwise unmatched combination of features, the FIA offers more stability than bonds with 40% to 60% of the upside potential of large-cap equities.

TABLE 8. THE FIA CAN OUT-PERFORM WHEN BONDS UNDER-PERFORM

Below Median and Above Median Bond Return Environments (1927-2016)

	Below Median Bond Return Environments Average Return	Above Median Bond Return Environments Average Return	Overall Period Average Return
Long Term Gov't Bonds	1.87%	9.00%	5.43%
Large Cap Stocks	11.43%	9.84%	10.63%
FIA	4.42%	7.55%	5.98%
60/40 (Stocks & Bonds)	7.60%	9.50%	8.55%
60/20/20 (Stocks, Bonds, & FIA)	8.12%	9.21%	8.66%
60/40 (Stocks & FIA)	8.63%	8.92%	8.77%

Source: 2017 SBBI Yearbook, Roger G. Ibbotson, Duff & Phelps; Zebra Capital; AnnGen Development, LLC

According to Ibbotson, the FIA's unique combination of features—elimination of downside risk while offering upside potential based on a portion of large-cap equity returns—qualifies it as an asset class in its own right, and renders it suitable to serve as a portfolio diversifier for wealth accumulation purposes. His white paper concludes that "an FIA may be an attractive alternative to traditional fixed income options like bonds to accumulate financial assets (tax-deferred) prior to retirement."

The FIA can be Designed to Generate Increasing Income

Consistent with Professor Ibbotson's focus, most FIAs today are described as safe wealth-accumulation vehicles that can diversify the stocks/bonds/cash paradigm that dominates the retirement investment narrative. But the key to appreciating the FIA's unique contribution to the stable-core portfolio is not solely its potential performance viewed through the historical lens of expected return.

Rather than using index-linked returns solely for accumulation purposes, the FIA can be designed to apply indexed interest to a stream of lifelong income. In doing so, it offers an advantage unmatched by any other asset class, and in my view seals its role as "retirement portfolio anchor."

Combining annual reset to a lifetime income guarantee hedging longevity risk is an actuarial benefit only an insurance company can offer. Some FIAs offer this benefit—either built-in or in the form of a rider includable for an additional fee—that increases lifetime income payments every year interest is credited. Establishing a new irreducible income floor with each increase, such FIAs epitomize their function as actuarial transformers of the option budget into increasing yield. The "increasing income" option competes as one of the most cost-effective responses to the inflation challenge available today. While level-payment annuity options might pay more at the outset, the increasing income option can "catch up" and potentially exceed a level payout over the course of an extended retirement.

Thus, not only can an FIA offer continuing mortality credits to help ensure that your paychecks never stop while you are alive, those mortality credits can continue to grow the annual payout. Figure 40 illustrates the hypothetical results if indexed income had been paid over the period from January 1, 2000-January 1, 2018 based on an annual reset and 40% participation rate.

FIGURE 40. HYPOTHETICAL FIA YIELD WHEN DESIGNED TO INCREASE LIFELONG INCOME BASED ON ANNUAL INTEREST CREDITS

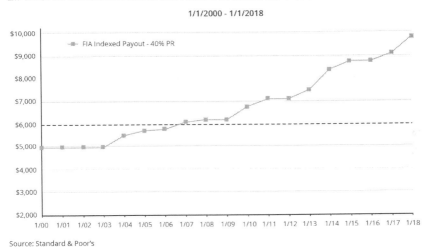

1/1/2000 - 1/1/2018

Source: Standard & Poor's

The FIA as Portfolio Anchor

As supported by Professor Ibbotson's findings, the FIA has a lot to offer retirees in our current economic environment. Insulating investors from potential market losses and smoothing returns, its use can drastically change investor psychology and behavior, improving long-term financial outcomes in the process simply by keeping policy owners invested. Savings allocated to the FIA are "safe," and yet it can be expected to deliver a higher return than the more traditional "safe" alternatives, like CDs and fixed annuities. As Ibbotson has pointed out, in a 3% bond environment, an FIA may also outperform long-term government bonds, without any of the downside risk presented by a rising-rate/declining-price environment. Unlike a traditional fixed annuity, the FIA offers investment flexibility: You are free to accept a share of coupon interest one year, and allocate to an equity-linked crediting formula the next.

While advantageous solely in an accumulation role, it is arguable that the FIA's highest and best use may be its ability to guarantee a lifetime of income. If you have the luxury of an accumulation phase before you trigger income, the holding period should give you enough experience and information to know if you will stay invested for the actuarial payoff. If you should decide not to, by the end of that gated period (when policy withdrawals greater than 10% per year should no longer trigger surrender charges), you should be able to walk away with your full accumulation value.

Which specific FIA, or combination of them, may work best for your situation is something for you to determine with your advisor. The same is true for its proportional allocation in your portfolio and the selection of any accompanying securities. To be done right, these choices should be made as part of a comprehensive retirement plan that considers not only the management of your financial assets, but also a myriad of other interrelated factors, including your liabilities and taxes, your Social Security benefit timing, your health and long-term care needs, your wealth transfer objectives, and your lifestyle goals.

Facing an uncertain future, where do *you* stand in your personal retirement process? Will the next ten years be a pre-retirement accumulation phase, the first decade of actual retirement, or the second or third decade of a retirement already underway? Will your retirement portfolio be called upon to weather a perfect storm or are these concerns overblown?

The good news for retirees and those planning for retirement is that the stable-core portfolio anchored to the Fixed Index Annuity is designed to protect and perform in either scenario, adapting to serve your accumulation goals and income needs in good times and bad. No matter your positioning, on both the retirement continuum and the wealth spectrum, there is no better time than the present to reset your strategy and tactics to optimally hedge whatever the future may have in store.

Takeaways

1. The FIA contract does not directly participate in any stocks or investments. You are not buying any bonds, shares of stock, or shares of an index fund. It's not possible to invest directly in an index. The market index value does not include dividends.

2. The FIA puts derivatives to work to generate higher policy returns without exposing policy values to market risk.

3. The FIA is a financial innovation, combining insurance guarantees together with a share of large cap equity-linked growth potential.

4. By means of derivatives, a fixed index annuity can now participate in the gains of common or synthetic market indices.

5. The FIA enables retirees to participate in upside market momentum without fear of ensnarement in a market correction or mean reversion.

Questions for your financial advisor

1. Do you know what an FIA is, how it's built and what it's pros and cons may be?

2. Have your clients ever invested in it and, if so, what was their experience, positive and negative?

3. How would their real-time results compare to the results harvested by investors in a balanced securities portfolio (like the one you're recommending) when measured over the same full market cycle?

4. I'm wary of the stock market but don't want to miss out. Do you think the FIA is worth considering for exposure to at least a portion of the market's upside potential?

5. Can you explain how the reset feature works and how positive index credits can grow my income without ever requiring a future giveback?

Chapter 10

HEDGED TO WIN

*Annuities have for a long time deserved a place
in retirement portfolios, and the evolution in the industry
has made these vehicles more flexible and attractive.
As with any investment, working with a trusted advisor... is key.*

Roger G. Ibbotson, PhD, Professor Emeritus of Finance,
Yale School of Management

Winning at retirement is first and foremost a matter of sustaining your desired lifestyle for as long as you live. If you are reading this book, you are likely nearing, entering or already engaged in the paycheck generating process. Having come this far, you recognize that your predominant retirement objective is not return, but yield— in the form of guaranteed lifelong cash flow that can increase to keep pace with inflation. Students of the retirement planning field, academic experts and most practitioners define winning quantitatively as simply not running out of the income you need—or the capital that generates that income—before you run out of time. In its most rudimentary economic form, retirement success is contrasted with retirement ruin, a condition given the mathematical definition displayed in Figure 41.

FIGURE 41. THE PROBABILITY OF RETIREMENT RUIN

$$\Pr[SVP > \omega] = \text{GammaDist} \left(\frac{2\mu + 4\lambda}{\sigma^2 + \lambda} - 1, \frac{\sigma^2 + \lambda}{2} \mid \frac{1}{\omega} \right) \quad (50)$$

If one is willing to assume lognormal returns in a continuous time setting, under μ, σ parameters and λ exponential mortality, the probability of retirement ruin is shown above. Where GammaDist(a β | .) dentoes the cumulative distribution function (CDF) of the Gamma distribution evaluated at the parameter pair α β .

In my opinion, a winning retirement is defined by much more than a mathematical equation. To truly succeed at retirement requires the cultivation of a winning mindset. Getting across the finish line that marks the end of your career victorious should affirm the psychological attitudes and spiritual values that enhance your *quality* of life. After decades of hard work and accomplishment, you can arrange your affairs to experience a retirement threatened by depletion, constrained by austerity and driven to hoarding, or as a phase of life that exudes confidence, licenses spending and encourages generosity. In an ideal scenario, retirees will enjoy the fruits of a life well lived, arranging their surplus to flow in unending abundance, to be shared with the people and causes they care about, furthering their life's larger purposes in the process. The key is to maximize capital efficiency to generate discretionary wealth to lavish on yourself and others.

My goal is to help you become (last) winners in retirement. Getting there requires an individualized application of the financial mechanics. Here are the basic principles.

Hedging (Essential!)

Some may find it comforting that in 2017 Janet Yellen, nearing the end of her term as Chairperson of the Federal Reserve, declared the end of financial panics, at least for the remaining duration of her lifetime. Others may be put off by the sheer hubris of her announcement, reminded of similarly self-assured but misguided pronouncements made by her predecessors. One of them is William White, the Swiss-based head of the review board of the Organization for Economic Cooperation and Development (OECD) and ex-Chief economist for the Bank for International Settlements (BIS). At the 2018 World Economic Forum in Davos, White cautioned that "all the market indicators right now look very similar to what we saw before the Lehman crisis, but the lesson has somehow been forgotten." Meanwhile, the latest stability report by the US Treasury's Office of Financial Research (OFR) warns that a mere 1% rise in the yield on 10-year US Treasuries—the world's benchmark price of money—would slash $1.2 trillion of value from the Barclays US Aggregate (Investment Grade) Bond Index, with additional losses suffered in lower-rated bonds, mortgages and derivative securities. And yet, at this writing, markets feel stress-free, which contrarians take as a very troubling sign.

Yellen's bold attitude stems from the heightened regulatory oversight and proactive interventionist orientation the Fed has adopted and evolved since at least Black Monday 1987. Expropriating the language of options, the willingness of the Fed to intervene in equity and bond markets (to sustain their prices and keep them from crashing) is referred to as the Greenspan "put." In 1987, the then-Fed Chairman pumped cash into the big money-center banks. That cash was intended to flow through to Wall Street broker/dealers to provide "liquidity" needed by investors to support demand for financial assets (bidding up their prices). Believing that an institutional "put" is in place emboldens investors to go 100% long, buying financial assets and betting on their ever-rising prices. A put is a derivative contract designed to protect market participants from losses incurred in a market collapse; a put makes money when the underlying security falls in value. The Fed's "institutional put" is designed to avert a market collapse in the first place, enticing investors to buy without fear of losses. It's one use for derivatives and an example of hedging.

Hedging is the practice of allocating a portion of your investment portfolio to "safer" or inversely correlated holdings that will protect you from market losses and/or position you to gain during a market downturn to offset losses in other parts of your portfolio. Hedges run a wide gamut:

Cash qualifies as a hedge because it will protect you from a stock or bond market rout, so portfolio managers raise cash when they see trouble coming. But cash imposes an opportunity cost because it could be earning more if it were invested in securities. When it earns very little and loses purchasing power to inflation, cash becomes a wasting asset. So as a hedge, cash (liquidity) can be expensive.

Diversification itself is a hedging technique. According to modern portfolio theory the bonds in your portfolio are intended to inversely correlate with your stocks to reduce portfolio losses by gaining or at least sustaining value when stocks fall. Rarely—if ever over the last 100 years—have bonds fully offset stock declines. On average, your allocation to bonds will earn barely half of what your stocks may earn in good years, so once again your diversification hedge reduces your overall return. Moreover, with the Fed signaling an impending return to higher rates, bonds could lose value in the months and years ahead. If those same rising rates trigger the long-awaited stock correction, both asset classes will fall in tandem and the "diversification" hedge will fail as it did in 2008, when practically all asset classes around the world dropped in unison, some more and some less.

Implementing **stop orders** is intended to limit losses by triggering a holding's sale once a pre-set limit down has been reached—but you need a buyer to stop a free fall. When markets crash, there are often no buyers at any price. Mutual funds designed to move inversely with the broader market, sometimes leveraged two-to-three-fold, can rise when markets fall. But when markets defy expectation, leveraged funds can lose value fast.

And then there are **derivatives**—puts and calls, options and futures—which are used to hedge adverse market outcomes by increasing in value when underlying long positions lose value. Many money managers recommend a portion of assets be used to implement an option overlay that hedges a portfolio's long positions. Derivatives are used as leveraged insurance "just in case;" very small premiums can multiply 10-20 times in value or more when markets swing wildly.

No matter the hedge, the process of hedging costs money, reducing the return on your overall portfolio. Classic hedge funds first emerged back in the late 1950s, serving wealthy investors willing to forego some upside precisely to avoid an unlimited drawdown in adverse markets. Their rationale was to intentionally trail the overall market in any one year, sacrificing return by spending on hedges to avoid a catastrophic market downdraft. By avoiding or minimizing losses, the hedge fund's long-term returns would be smoothed, enabling the investor to stay invested and end up (after a *full* market cycle) earning enough return to meet objectives—but with much less volatility and risk. Hedge funds have since developed a reputation for out-performance; their founders now specialize in market timing and/or asset classes and proprietary investment strategies that seek to earn more than the broad markets and generate returns even when the broad markets fail. Highly specialized, hedge funds charge annual fees of 2% to 3%, plus 20% or more of annual profits, and their clients are happy to pay these fees when they outperform. Alas, as regularly reported in the Wall Street Journal since the dawn of the "new normal" in 2008, hedge funds have been closing their doors in droves because even their alternative strategies and tactics have failed to earn out.

The reality is, since the GFC, nothing much has worked consistently in the realm of active management. According to the 2016 SPIVA® US Scorecard published by S&P Dow Jones Indices, almost 90% of active stock managers failed to beat their index targets over the previous 10-year period, with fees of 1% or so accounting for a significant part of that underperformance. What *has* worked? Low-cost, passive investing using robotic ETFs designed to replicate an index, an approach that has become increasingly popular among do-it-yourself/price-sensitive retirees. Passive investing is long only; it prospers when asset prices rise, but offers no downside protection. Un-hedged and requiring barely any manager skill, passive investing is therefore inexpensive. The tradeoff? In a scenario where investors panic and rush to the exits, ETFs could be hit hard.

Trailing the indices and the low-cost funds that hug them, many of today's tried-and-true money managers find themselves caught between a rock and a hard place. Recognizing their fiduciary responsibility to protect as well as grow client assets, many have lagged their benchmarks. This change has occurred precisely because they have hedged their exposure, either by raising cash, increasing fixed-income allocations, reducing or avoiding exposure to certain stocks, and/or implementing carefully structured derivative overlays designed to recover at least some of the portfolio value that could be lost in a crash.

Hedging in one or more of these ways has cost these managers dearly in terms of risk-adjusted returns, client loyalty and their bread-and-butter assets under management (AUM). Legendary financial industry thought leaders critical of today's long-only index-hugging securities portfolio wrack their brains to come up with "outside-the-box" investing styles to distinguish themselves from their competitors and outperform without exposing clients to the full brunt of catastrophic losses possible should market forces ever overwhelm central bank support. Concerned about volatility— whether too much or too little—these experienced technicians plumb their know-how to devise unconventional security selection strategies and esoteric timing signals that, in combination, mitigate risk *and* capture return.

Why do these proven asset managers go to such heroic lengths to justify market exposure in the face of perceived risk? They do it because what shapes their mindset is the fundamental article of faith perhaps best articulated by Howard Marks, founder and CIO of Oaktree Capital: "There are actually two risks in investing: One is to lose money and the other is to miss opportunity. You can eliminate either one, but you can't eliminate both at the same time."

Marks' pronouncement is true if your product allocations are limited to securities and your objective is risk-adjusted return.

As a retiree, isn't it ironic that your primary purpose in chasing returns today is to convert them to yield? Given today's economic uncertainties, securities—with their attendant volatility—are not well suited to this purpose. Can you stay in stocks and bear the risk of being interminably ensnared in a grinding market collapse? Can you stay in cash and bear the certainty of eroded purchasing power magnified by the possibility of missed upside potential? Can you commit to bonds for safe returns with a rising-rate environment looming?

It is important to remember that you are not just an investor. You are a retiree facing an additional set of entirely different risks that also need hedging, including longevity, return-sequence, depletion and inflation. What makes the fixed index annuity the optimal hedge for *you* is that while it protects you from market losses, it also guarantees you a lifelong cash flow enhanced to reflect actuarial mortality credits, while potentially increasing year over year thanks to annual credits earned from equity market exposure.

But will there be anything left for your heirs?

Legacy Planning (Not necessarily)

As conventionally portrayed, retirement planning is often conflated with legacy planning. The disposition of your estate is said to be one of the three "L's" that make up a set of intertwined goals that include: 1) Lifestyle funding, 2) Liquidity provision, and 3) Legacy creation.

Whether you can afford to leave wealth to your descendants—assuming you are so inclined—emerges in the retirement planning process. In my experience, many clients feel they have already sacrificed for their children—as evidenced by diminished savings spent on expensive educations, ongoing college debt service, or continuing support for children and grandchildren. For these individuals, it is clear from the start that legacy goals barely make their priority list. Others recognize instinctively that their finite assets simply aren't sufficient to do double-duty for multiple generations, while a few may be willing to consider the cost-benefit tradeoffs entailed but usually on a non-committal basis.

And yet, in the academic literature as well as in conventional advisory practice, legacy creation is regularly given the same level of importance as lifestyle funding and liquidity provision. I often wonder why. In a way, it's redolent of earlier times, when retirees could "live off the interest" earned by their savings, painlessly preserving principal for descendants. In an era of financial repression that simple formula no longer works, because low yields mandate that principal be invaded to generate needed income. Or, in the obverse, prioritizing an estate for heirs significantly reduces spending. For example: At this writing, 2% is the projected yield on a safe 30-year "bond ladder," a portfolio of sequenced bonds timed to mature each year to match your cash flow needs to avoid having to sell any at the wrong time and incur a loss. A 65-year-old couple with a $1 million nest egg planning for a 30-year joint life expectancy funded by such a bond ladder can spend down at a level rate of $43,775 per year, leaving nothing at the end. If you want $500,000 to remain, you must reduce your annual spending by 28%, to $31,690 per year. If you want to leave your entire million-dollar nest egg intact, you'll have to reduce annual spending by 55% to $19,600. Those annual reductions in your income can be thought of as the "cost" of your bequest motive.

But wait. If your portfolio could earn more than 2%, wouldn't your austerity burden be lessened? Why not add equities to your asset mix, because historically they've delivered higher average annual returns than cash or bonds? Indeed, if the future is anything like the past, increasing stocks to 50% of your asset allocation could enhance your total portfolio return to 5% to 8%, and may even leave you richer instead of depleted thirty years from now! "You *do* want the stock market to make you richer, don't you?" goes the classic inquiry.

And that's the point: Including equities in a balanced retirement portfolio is done to benefit future generations just as much as to enhance your withdrawals 2% to 3% by cashing in (hopefully) appreciated securities each year to top up what you would be earning from your bond ladder alone.

Hence, one reason legacy creation has become such an integral component of retirement planning is that it's dependent on a portfolio's stock allocation. In a low-return environment, fixed-income bonds and annuities are destined to be spent down; if anything's going to be left after 30 to 40 years, it would have to come from the growth potential unique to stocks. So, goes the argument, the greater your bequest motive, the greater your proportional allocation to equities should be; an indelible logic that makes Wall Street advisers big proponents of investment-driven estate planning and "family wealth" management.

A connected but not uncontested claim added to the argument is that the longer the time horizon, the less risky the long-run return on stocks, rendering the projected value of the ultimate bequest more dependable. What gets overlooked is that an estate can often be created with greater certainty and lower cost using tax-free life insurance, while market volatility and adverse return sequence can combine to vastly undermine the end result.

In the same vein, there's no guarantee that enhanced retirement cash flow will result from a proposed equity allocation. It depends on the return sequence started on the day you choose to retire. Who knows if the future is going to be like the past or, for that matter, what period in the past it may emulate? The emphasis on growth in a retirement portfolio, therefore, can be misleading—unless applied to income.

First and foremost, your retirement portfolio should be focused on securing guaranteed lifetime income sufficient to sustain a lifestyle made up of both needs-based and discretionary spending. That's why, to the disappointment of some stock advocates, the performance of a true retirement portfolio is rightly measured in terms of yield—the income it generates—rather than return—the gains and losses it accrues from year to year. Until pre-empted by the Wall Street narrative in the early 1990s, retirement planning was always couched in terms of guaranteed income.

The reality is that introducing stock-based growth into a retirement income portfolio can end up in direct conflict with the income objective and actually undermine it. Guaranteed retirement income is simply not Wall Street's strength, nor has it ever been. As a matter of law, investment firms cannot guarantee results; as a matter of practice, they focus gains on relatively short-term outcomes; and as a standard of performance, they measure success in terms of growth-based total return, not yield.

Nevertheless, over the past thirty years the Wall Street balanced portfolio has come to be considered the default for sophisticated retirement money in both the pre-retirement accumulation phase, as well as in the post-retirement spend-down phase. Surprisingly, the diversified portfolio's use as a retirement income solution was never the intent of Professor Harry Markowitz, the developer of Modern Portfolio Theory (MPT). Recognized for calculating the complex mathematical parameters of portfolio construction, MPT won Markowitz the Nobel Prize in Economics and continues to define Wall Street's approach to asset allocation, correlation and diversification.

The MPT method seeks to combine assets with complementary characteristics—like stocks and bonds—along an efficient frontier that delivers maximum return per unit of accompanying risk. Guided by historical mathematical relationships, it combines asset classes in specific ratios to maximize year-by-year risk-adjusted return. The 60/30/10 balanced portfolio offered by Wall Street as its generic retirement solution is built on this theory. But in 1991, Markowitz announced that he never intended MPT to be applied to retirement planning. Rather, he revealed, "an evening of reflection convinced me that there were key differences in the central features of investment for institutions and investment for individuals."

His work, he clarified, was intended for large institutional investors with unlimited life spans and zero withdrawal requirements. Human beings with finite life spans who need to fund spending by tapping their portfolios faced a sequence of return risk that could trigger literal ruin—a far more complicated problem than MPT presumed to address or dared to solve!

An MPT-based investment portfolio may work well enough during a pre-defined accumulation period when withdrawals don't drain assets and an average return over a long time horizon can achieve a predictable end result no matter the actual sequence of returns. It's in the indeterminate decumulation phase—the retirement spending phase—that new challenges emerge and proliferate, such as losses compounded by withdrawals. According to its developer, the underlying theory of modern investing simply does not address those retirement spend-down challenges.

This begs the question of why Wall Street advisors insist that the balanced portfolio remains the optimal solution and are only begrudgingly willing to reduce a portfolio's stock allocation to accommodate an aging client's grumpy risk aversion. In his epochal research seeking the safemax withdrawal rate, industry thought leader William Bengen studied the 20th Century performance of a portfolio evenly distributed between stocks and bonds—replicating his own holdings and the portfolio approach he recommended to clients—because his MPT-portfolio bias inclined him to assume that no other viable option existed. He reconfirmed that bias a decade later, when he announced that follow-up research had led him to conclude that a 75% allocation to stocks might in fact be optimal, thereby providing authoritative confirmation for professionals who focus on stocks.

The Stock Bias

When conferring with financial advisors, it's important to keep in mind that they are subject to the same behavioral quirks and mental biases as the rest of us. When it comes to the balanced portfolio, overconfidence in the efficacy of stocks is endemic; recency bias expressed in blue-sky expectations of perpetual stock price increases is built-in; and herding revealed through policy portfolios that differ very little from firm to firm is the norm. Like the rest of us, investment advisors and portfolio managers tend to select their information to confirm what they already know to be true.

On Wall Street, stocks and returns are a religion. Living with investment risk and in the business of enrolling clients to take it on, the financial industry has developed a very unique bias that informs its advice. It may sound something like this: Since all markets are cyclical and revert to the mean, all portfolios (especially if bought high) eventually suffer losses—although they can be: 1) reduced by application of the diversification principals elucidated in Modern Portfolio Theory, and 2) temporary (we hope) based on historical precedent. Losses are nevertheless baked into the cake and there's nothing you can do about it, so they simply must be endured for the sake of greater wealth in the long run. In fact, it might even be said that it's only thanks to losses that risk assets deliver the compensatory excess returns. *Losses are nothing but the price a savvy investor occasionally pays in the short run to earn the risk premium in the long run, and an informed, bold risk-taker can be expected to grin and bear them.* Therefore, investment risk, though it may keep you up at night, is inherently a good thing and in retirement you will be too astute to let it ruin you. If need be, you'll just tighten your belt—temporarily compromising your lifestyle—until your retirement asset pool inevitably recovers.

It's easy to say. And while some financial advisors can be remarkably cavalier when it comes to imposing austerity on clients—expecting them to reduce their lifestyles by spending less when markets turn down and portfolios lose value—why is austerity ever needed? It's because the stock-centric model of wealth accumulation is nourished—and starved—by volatility. Its market-based method-ology holds you—the investor—hostage to its risky unpredictability. Your spending goals may have to be sacrificed to the markets' vagaries and you are likely to overshoot on the abstemious side leaving assets on the table, but that's just the way it is.

Ergo, you're beset with endless messaging that if you want to be smart about "managing your wealth" you really have no choice but to learn to live with uncertainty. That advice is usually followed by some version of the classic regulatory disclaimer: *Investing involves risk, including in the worst case a total and permanent loss of your principal. Past performance is no guarantee of future results. Invest wisely.*

The traditional wealth accumulation process is not the focus of "Modern Retirement Theory" because, for one thing, the true measure of retirement success is not building an estate for heirs. Rather, it's the enjoyment of spendable income sufficient to sustain your lifestyle (needs *and* wants) come what may, for however long you may live—together with the added security of a liquid contingency reserve to cover emergencies. Any resources remaining after allocating what's needed to fund those two essential purposes can be considered discretionary, available to spend, invest, donate or even (go ahead) gamble away.

Retirement risk, in other words, should not be thought of solely in terms of investment risk. Recovery from losses incurred in the wealth accumulation phase, for example, requires time and patience; recovery from portfolio losses once withdrawals are underway requires urgency and sacrifice. Belt-tightening in response to portfolio losses equates to reducing current and future consumption to protect remaining portfolio value from now-accelerated depletion. But your withdrawals aren't elective, used for reinvesting to grow your wealth; rather, they sustain your lifestyle by funding your spending goals. Reduced withdrawals mean lifestyle shortfalls that can be constricting at best, and painful at worst.

Considering the mathematics of loss, it would be fair to worry, in such circumstances, about ever recovering enough to get back on track and resume your prior level of spending. If you don't, you will be facing a permanent reduction in your standard of living. Losing money while you are spending down can have spiraling lifestyle consequences for you and your loved ones.

Irony Alert: Wall Street Proposes a Do-It-Yourself Annuity

By aiming to generate a series of cash flows from a specific mix of stocks and bonds until all income and capital are spent, the Wall Street securities portfolio actually seeks to emulate a point-in-time-designated-certain (usually 30-year) income annuity—absent any real insurance guarantees. Instead, it relies upon a "Systematic Withdrawal Plan" (SWiP) and the willingness of the investor to withdraw (and live on) less if necessary to prevent premature depletion.

However, writing for The CFA Institute Research Foundation, York University Professor of Mathematics, Statistics and Finance Moshe Milevsky, PhD, pointed out that "A SWiP is a (dumb) mechanical liquidation rule that extracts a fixed amount of cash from a retirement portfolio by selling assets to create a desired level of income, regardless of the price level of markets. So, for example, if a retiree implements a SWiP for $50,000 per year and, in one particular year, the dividends and interest from the portfolio are (only) $20,000, then $30,000 worth of securities are sold to make up the income difference. Under a SWiP, the systematic sale of $30,000 worth of securities ignores fundamental valuation levels and any other market-timing rules. It is the mirror image of dollar-cost averaging, under which a fixed amount of money is invested in securities on a regular basis independent of valuation levels. Although many individuals view SWiPs as an alternative to life annuities, a SWiP can fully deplete whereas a life annuity cannot. The GLWB offers a SWiP with some insurance protection—namely, that if the account value ever hits zero as a result of the depletions, the insurance company will continue paying the annuity."

Wall Street's do-it-yourself annuity turns clients into "guessing" annuitizers who must reduce annual withdrawals in the face of negative returns if they want to prevent premature depletion. That's because a bank can't pool actuarial risks to put a floor under the payout, enhance the initial yield, or fund mortality credits. To exceed a 2% payout rate, the bank must resort to equities to increase total return, imposing all the attendant risks on the portfolio owner. In contrast, an insurer relies on actuarial science to enhance yield beyond the underlying 2% it may earn for the policyholder while absorbing all the risks involved in that process.

Rendering the Wall Street method even less competitive today is the prospect of mean-reverting returns from equities for the next decade or two. The securities portfolio has to produce returns to pay out its 4%. The life annuity can earn 2% and make up the difference using the mortality credits that actuarial science harvests in the process of longevity risk pooling.

The need to accept the risk of outliving the Wall Street portfolio is another key detriment to this approach. The classic policy portfolio tested by thought leader William Bengen (and now widely accepted by the financial industry) had a limited time horizon; it was designed to deplete at the end of thirty years. That time horizon more than covers the life expectancy of most males and females now at age 65, but misses an unknown number of individuals who are likely to live past age 95. What are you supposed to do after spending down to zero? The insured life annuity pays you for as long as you survive. Its payout stream cannot be outlived, and that's the whole idea.

Moreover, the securities-centric advisor community concedes that its approach will likely leave some do-it-yourself annuitizers out in the cold (even if they don't make it a full thirty years) should they be unlucky enough to run into an adverse return sequence. Relying only on uncontrollable probabilities, the Bengen approach is based on the premise of an "acceptable" failure rate of 10%. Failure in this context means ruin—unless you pre-empt it by tightening your belt, maybe for the duration of your retirement.

Thousands of Monte Carlo simulations calculate the likelihood of failure based on a given asset allocation and the inputs chosen to set expectations for returns, correlations and combinations. Because of the subjectivity involved in setting those parameters, the Monte Carlo approach is criticized for overstating the odds of success and understating the odds of failure. Even using historic averages, a 4% withdrawal rate adjusted annually for inflation may fail 10% of the time. As we've seen, though, inputting lower return expectations projects a 50% failure rate at 4%; only by reducing withdrawals to around 2.5% would the probability of success be restored to the 90% that is considered reasonable.

Would you be willing to accept even a 10% probability of failure? Possibly. How about a 50% chance of failure? The insured annuity guarantees success at 100% in any and all scenarios. Using the risk pool for actuarial leverage, it can pay out 4% or more from inception with the assurance that it will pay you for as long as you live.

With stocks removed from the retirement equation, we are left with bonds as a possible core portfolio holding. The risk of rising rates—possibly triggering a bond market crash—puts a damper on our enthusiasm to build a plan solely or primarily on a bond ladder. The portfolio would have no appreciation potential unless interest rates were to fall further into negative territory. The payout from such a portfolio would stay level, losing purchasing power to relentless inflation—especially as it relates to the cost of healthcare. As important as its potentially competitive return, it's the risks currently associated with bonds in a retirement portfolio that provide market-sage Roger Ibbotson his two-pronged rationale for recommending they be replaced at least for now by the FIA.

Anchoring the retirement portfolio to an FIA core provides a competitive level of initial minimum income in the 4% to 5% range, comprising a non-reducible floor. The FIA also offers dynamic investment flexibility. It can capture a share of various asset class returns to earn interest credits that, in some arrangements, can increase the level of cash flow year to year. This can help retirees keep pace with—or even sometimes exceed—the rate of inflation. The lifetime withdrawal benefit assures an unfailing stream of income. The policy's underlying guarantees are backed by the reserve-and-surplus-based claims-paying ability of the issuer, buttressed by the regulatory apparatus, business practices and economic incentives built into the modern insurance industry.

Portfolio Construction

How much of your nest egg should be dedicated to the FIA? Here's my recommended approach:

Step 1. **Calculate** your run rate. From the adjusted gross income reported on your most recent tax returns subtract the federal, state and local income taxes you paid and any contributions to savings, before tax or after. Unless you are dipping into your assets, the result is the annual "burn rate" that sustains your current standard of living. If you are also spending capital, add your annual spend-down to the initial burn rate to calculate your gross cost of living. Now add back the taxes you pay. The total is your "gross number," the total amount of annual cash flow you need.

Step 2. **Inventory** your assets and potential income sources. These can include Social Security benefits payable now and/or at full retirement age or at age 70; pensions payable now and at full retirement age; full or part-time earned income that can continue through age 70 or later; any passive income receivable in the form of royalties, rents or renewal commissions and the like; pending gifts and any expected inheritances and their timing; financial assets—pre-tax "qualified" and after-tax "non-qualified"—that comprise your nest egg.

Step 3. **Quantify** the cost of guaranteeing the income needed to fund your current lifestyle by dividing total from Step 1 by 5%, the approximate payout you can expect from an FIA. For example, if your gross number is $100,000, the FIA needed to fund it would require a premium of approximately $2 million (.05 / 100,000 = 2,000,000).

Is your nest egg equal to, or worth more than $2 million? If it's the latter, consider deploying $2 million to lock in and assure the lifetime cash flow you require. Any leftover surplus can now be deployed to additional emergency liquidity or standalone legacy maximization, if desired, since its diminution or loss would not impact your retirement lifestyle.

If your financial nest egg is less than or equal to the required premium, start to reduce your gross number by activating your other income sources, such as your Social Security benefits, pension benefits, rents or royalties, gifts receivable, etc. to derive a net income requirement. Divide that number by 5% to determine how much of your nest egg would have to be deployed to generate it. Do you have enough? Do you have more than enough? If not, you may have to begin the process of actively reducing your cost of living by differentiating your essential needs from your discretionary wants, and/or making lifestyle changes. Then, start again at Step 2.

Step 4. **Trigger** your FIA cash flows. Don't defer them. Turning retirement scarcity into retirement abundance, the annuity can be a license to spend without guilt or fear. Maximizing its utility turns the Wall Street model (rooted in anxiety and austerity) on its head. Consume your premium and its earnings as rapidly as the contract allows, so you can get to the risk pool funded by other people's money. Spending OPM enhances your rate of return, so get to it. In addition, in your new generous mindset, turn on your Social Security benefits whether you need them or not; who knows how much will be there for you in the future? (Who knows if *you* will be there to collect what's coming to you?) The same is true for your pension. Trigger it. Use those three sources to create cash flow abundance, freeing yourself from abstemious scarcity. Ideally, all other sources of income now become "surplus." If you don't need to spend them, bank them, pay down debt, or give them away to family members or your favorite charities.

By making the FIA the core of your portfolio, you will secure a self-sufficient, independent retirement. Unless you need your supplementary cash flows to reach your gross number, spend because your economy needs you and it's the patriotic thing to do. Pursue the coveted promise conveyed in Mr. Spock's Vulcan blessing: Live Long and Prosper.

Step 5. **Allocate** your surplus assets and don't be afraid to put your cash flows to work. Spend. Gift. Donate. Invest.

Thus, in my approach, portfolio construction *begins* with your allocation to the FIA anchor, your core retirement asset, because it alone provides the cash flow reliability and predictability you can count on. Only the FIA *guarantees* lifelong cash flows *you own*. All other sources—Social Security, pensions, royalties, rents, corporate dividends, bond interest, capital gains, etc.—are subject to exogenous forces out of your control that could reduce, interrupt or stop their flows entirely.

But the FIA can't comprise your entire portfolio. Allocate to it only the portion of your nest egg needed to deliver the level of retirement security you crave, leaving the remainder for allocation to cash and other forms of insurance—and then securities—that can play important supporting roles.

True Liquidity

After your FIA allocation, your most important portfolio consideration is liquidity. True liquidity is what is left after you subtract the cost of your income guarantee from your available financial assets. Importantly, true liquidity — the ability (at any time) to convert an asset into cash for the price originally paid for it—eludes the Wall Street portfolio. Other than its relatively small cash component, its stocks and bonds are volatile, their prices rising and falling to reflect market forces. Stocks and bonds are "marketable," meaning they can usually (though not always) find buyers at *some* price, but they are not "liquid" in the proper sense (that without fail, they will find buyers for the price you paid for them).

The Wall Street portfolio is illiquid in another key sense as well: exceptional gains achieved in any given year cannot be cashed in and withdrawn; withdrawals from the portfolio must be limited to the underlying income budget (say, 4% of the starting balance increased annually by inflation) even when a given year's return might far exceed the long-term averages. This is because excess gains must be preserved to give back when markets take them back in years when proportional losses are suffered. Preserving outsized gains to give back is the only way to sustain a portfolio's asset value at a level consistent with its long-term targeted average return. In other words, for all its advertised performance potential, the Wall Street portfolio in retirement is actually quite stingy, averse to freeing up any excess returns without increasing the risk of premature depletion and imposing indeterminate belt-tightening.

Meanwhile, Fidelity Investment's 2015 Retiree Health Care Cost Estimate cautions that at least $245,000 should be set aside by the average couple age 65 just to cover out-of-pocket medical expenses likely to be incurred over the remainder of their lives. That sum can't come from the cash component of your income portfolio. It has to come from genuine surplus apart from the income portfolio itself.

Rendering Surplus Productive

Since cash flow is king in retirement, I recommend that the first tranche of any surplus should be rendered productive (i.e., of income) while incurring as little market risk to principal as possible.

After market risk, personal risk takes another two forms when it comes to retirement planning: risk tolerance and risk capacity. The former measures your psychological predisposition for suffering in proportion to financial loss; the latter measures the amount of loss you can endure before having to cut back on tangible spending. Your risk tolerance is a key element of the Wall Street portfolio design process, but once in retirement, almost *all* losses tend to be experienced very negatively. In light of this, we work on the assumption that, in the real world, once retired you have almost zero tolerance for loss—especially if it results in reduced cash flow.

If you have risk capacity, however, you might include an equity exposure—not necessarily for its dividend payout (you would no longer be relying solely or even primarily on dividends to provide you with income)—but for the long-term appreciation potential it can offer. For the more prudent investor, a value-based approach that seeks to buy stocks at discounts from their intrinsic value may be ideal. If your goal is legacy creation, you might consider a more volatile group of small-cap stocks. Over an open-ended time horizon, small companies have been shown to offer the highest growth potential.

Keep in mind, though, that if your goal is truly intergenerational wealth transfer and you're in reasonably good health, you may find that tax-free life insurance offers a less risky approach than a long-term equity allocation. Specifically, survivorship life policies that insure both spouses under one umbrella should be properly evaluated. At the same time, any possible need for individual coverage to protect a spouse should not be ignored. It may be invaluable in replacing Social Security, pension or part-time income lost at death. The assumption that life insurance is no longer needed once you enter retirement can be misleading.

Meeting ongoing insurance needs is both a very productive use for surplus cash flows, and an important reason for generating them. In a holistic retirement portfolio, long-term care coverage is one of the most important of these needs. Actuarial studies predict that over 70% of retirees will need long-term care services at some point, and the expenses involved can be a major drain on assets and a drag on income. If an annual premium allocation to long-term care coverage isn't a part of your retirement expense budget, it should be. Since men tend to incur the expenses before women, the coverage is designed to protect the residual portfolio for the surviving spouse. It's an indispensable wealth-preservation tool that tends to go under-utilized by investment advisors.

Your Retirement Reset

To generate and sustain a competitive level of income without fear of depletion no matter how long you may live, my FIA-anchored stable-core portfolio is built around insurance rather than securities. It requires a conceptual reset rooted in a very different mindset—one that focuses on retirement spending—leaving securities in a supportive, but secondary role. Rather than imposing austerity that tends to be overdone, the FIA-centered mindset incentivizes spending and can transform retirement from a period of fearful hoarding into one of enlightened giving. Taking your values across the finish line, the freedom to contribute embodies the very essence of a winning retirement.

To a large extent, your success in retirement depends on your advisor's opinions and guidance, so be sure he or she has the expertise and experience necessary. Advanced financial-planning education can be a huge advantage, while a decent measure of common sense never hurts. Also, you'll want to clarify how your advisor is paid: a lot is made these days about commission-based vs. fee-based compensation. Some clients believe one form of compensation invites more conflicts of interest than the other, and it is important to be aware.

Do your standard due diligence, but don't stop there. Be sure to elicit your advisor's view, and the underlying perspectives that shape any recommendations. In the big picture, does your advisor's approach accept the possibility of decades-long financial repression, secular stagnation and a painful reversion of the mean in equity markets, or does it assume that stocks have nowhere to go but up, always recover quickly and belong in a dominant position at the center of your portfolio? Is it focused on maximal wealth accumulation, or does it recognize the wisdom of earning less—but enough—in the interest of hedging? Determine whether your advisor is comfortable only with the language of securities, or if she is equally comfortable with the language of insurance and actuarial science. Finally, probe to ascertain if the person in whose hands you may place your future is a real fiduciary—someone who puts your interests first by instinct and breeding, and not just by regulatory fiat.

Then ask yourself: If not now, when?

Takeaways

1. Even individuals with wherewithal at retirement cannot afford to lose money without having to make painful compromises to their lifestyles that could end up being permanent.

2. A historically overpriced stock market threatens to impose heavy losses in the form of an inevitable mean reversion, preceded and followed by below-average returns, possibly for an extended period.

3. Recovery from those losses may not come easily because adverse US demographics, like Japan's, may have already baked in a long period of economic stagnation ahead that could doom a recovery to decades.

4. Growing government debt worsens our nation's burden, possibly necessitating a decades-long period of financial repression, with government bonds earning little "nominal" and even less "real" return.

5. Cash may remain a wasting asset for as far as our dimming eyes can see.

Questions for your financial advisor

1. How can I participate in stock market momentum without risking retirement ruin?

2. How do you hedge your recommended portfolio against sudden shocks and potentially unrecoverable losses?

3. Will I have to bear the cost of market setbacks by reducing my lifestyle spending?

4. What do you know about the FIA and its potential role as the anchor of a stable-core income-focused retirement portfolio?

5. Once my investment plan is implemented, can you help me with my complementary insurance and estate planning needs?

Appendix I

THE RETIREMENT INCOME PLANNING DUALITY

	INSURANCE	BANKING
INTERMEDIARY	Insurer	Banker
MANDATE	Maximize Lifetime Spending	Maximize Lifetime Accumulation
PARADIGM	Modern Retirement Theory	Modern Portfolio Theory
MODALITY	Efficient Wealth Decumulation	Maximum Wealth Accumulation
LEGACY OBJECTIVE	Non-Essential/Incidental	Essential/Definitional
SUCCESS MEASURE	Guaranteed Plan Realization	Acceptable Probability of Plan Failure
LONGEVITY HORIZON	Open-Ended	Closed-Ended
RISK OF RUIN	Lifted	Looming
POSSIBLE SHORTFALL	Exposed to Runaway Inflation	Exposed to Market Losses and Inflation
PRIMARY METRIC	Yield	Returns
CASH FLOWS	Predictable	Un-Predictable
INCOME STREAM	Secure, Stable, Sustainable	Volatile, Risk of Permanent Reductions
RETURN OBJECTIVE	Enough to Meet Lifestyle Needs	More than Needed to Sustain Lifestyle
SPENDING RESPONSE	License to Maximize Early	Motivation to Over-Conserve
MARKET RISK	Shunned	Sought
RISK APPETITE	Little to None/Averse	Accepting to Eager/Resigned
MARKET DRAWDOWNS	Never	Regular
DRAWDOWN POTENTIAL	Zero	Unlimited
SEQUENCE RISK	Eliminated	Proportional to Equity Allocation
LEGAL STATUS	Contractual	Precautionary
RESULTS	Promissory	Non-Promissory
TRUE LIQUIDITY	More	Less
WITHDRAWAL RATES	Actuarially Determined	Safemax
OUTCOME	Guaranteed at Worst	Probable at Best
MINIMUM OUTCOME	Certain	Uncertain
PRIMARY METHODOLOGY	Asset-Liability Matching	Risk-Adjusted Total Return
INSTRUMENTATION	Fixed Index Annuity	The Balanced Portfolio
UPSIDE CAPTURE VIA	Leveraged Derivatives	Stocks for the Long Run
UPSIDE PARTICIPATION	Limited	Unlimited
ANNUAL PERFORMANCE	Likely to Trail Averages	May Beat Averages
SOURCE/EXCESS RETURN	Compensated Risk Pooling	Compensated Risk Taking
PREMIUM PURSUED	Mortality	Equity
FORECAST TOOL	Actuarial Science	Monte Carlo Simulation
CAPITAL EXPOSURE	Risk of Temporary Inconvenience	Risk of Permanent Impairment
CONSUMER CLAIMS ON	Capital & Reserves	B/D Best Efforts
INVESTOR EDGE	Index-Linked Credits	Manager Skill
MANAGEMENT STYLE	Passive: Participate, Integrate,	Active: Trade, Time, Select, Weight

Appendix II

RISKS, REMEDIES AND RESPONSES

I hate annuities and you should too.
Ken Fisher
CIO, Fisher Investments

The FIA gets criticized from many quarters and its limitations and risks need to be fully recognized and fairly addressed before you invest. Here are the ones you will likely hear and read about most often.

Any FIA's real risk is the magnitude and consistency of its future returns. Traditional fixed annuities provide predictable returns to the investor based on interest rates. These interest rates pay positive returns every year that the investor remains invested. An FIA crediting method offers returns only when market action favors it;

otherwise the investor receives 0%. Although most FIAs offer minimum guarantees, they do so only over the life of the FIA contract, which means you would have to stay invested at least for the duration of any surrender charge period to enjoy their modest benefit. What if the stock market drops and keeps dropping or, worse, stays flat for many years? Anything is possible, so I recommend FIAs that offer a fixed interest option together with index crediting methodologies. That way, in a worst-case scenario, you can revert to straightforward interest crediting until market action improves. Your annual interest should actually be pretty competitive and you don't have to lock in for the duration of the underlying bonds to earn it, hence you take no downside risk.

This performance concern also highlights the fact that it's market action that drives FIA returns and not the absolute values reached by any index. It's an index' relative increase from a given starting point that the FIA transforms into "excess credits." So if a market index drops 30% one year, your principal is preserved. To recover that loss the following year we know that the index would need to rise about 42%. If it did you would be expected to capture a share of that (or any) gain that would in turn be credited to your protected accumulation value, further increasing it and not just recovering what you may have lost. Thus, the FIA prospers on volatility and starves without it. Fortunately, market history attests to the fact that even in bearish periods (like the depression) stock markets still rose and fell; it's from that cyclicality that the FIA reaps its gains, theoretically making it an optimal holding for a bear market.

It also underscores a key difference between the traditional fixed annuity and the FIA. The traditional fixed annuity is a passive holding. It pays what it pays for its duration and there's no way you can get it to pay more or less. FIA performance can benefit from active policy owner management. On policy anniversaries, choices can be made about index allocations for the coming year: what methodology should be weighted, which index might offer the most upside potential, what blend of indices offers the best balance? Happily, you can make these choices without fear of making an irrecoverable mistake: worst case, you might earn less than what you could have had you—and your advisor—been better attuned and more astute.

Then there are those pesky caps, spreads and participation rates that are said to limit your earning power. You will hear that they constrain your upside potential, and that's usually true for any given year. The compensating impact of loss avoidance on your average long-term performance, however, tends to be overlooked. By locking in annual returns and avoiding stock market declines, you don't need to capture large upside market swings to "keep up" or recover losses, especially in the withdrawal phase of retirement when loss recovery is even further hamstrung by portfolio distributions. I often wonder exactly which S&P 500 returns you may be chasing: the thirty year average of 5.25% from 1954 to 1984, the 5.79% average annual return from 1964 to 1994, or the 10.05% average from 1974 to 2004?

While adverse market forces may limit returns, management discretion may have an even larger adverse impact. While bond yields and the price of call options affect index participation, the ultimate determining factor in future years is what carrier management decides to do when it declares renewal rates. Be sure to review the renewal history and audited financials of any company you are considering. You don't want your earning potential crippled by past management missteps that need to be corrected by increasing profits squeezed out of policy owner risk budgets!

As unlikely as it may be, in a worst-case scenario an insurance carrier you choose may go out of business. So far, no FIA buyer is known to have ever lost any money in a company failure. That's because no company offering FIAs has been known to fail, at least as of this writing. Nevertheless, to hedge this risk it may makes sense to diversify your FIA portfolio among several issuers.

The lack of liquidity attributable to surrender charges is another hot button when criticism is leveled at the FIA. It's true: an FIA is not an appropriate vehicle for assets that must remain truly liquid. Keep those in a bank or money market fund. But don't forget that almost all FIAs offer annual 10% surrender-charge-free withdrawals. Compare that to the 2% to 4% safemax limit your current Systematic Withdrawal Program imposes! A 10% withdrawal privilege should not hamstring most retirees. And should you need that 10% withdrawal, you can get it from the insurer without having to sell your personal bond holdings into what could be a rising interest rate environment for less than you may have paid for them. Selling assets from your balanced Wall Street portfolio risks liquidation losses. The insurance company absorbs that liquidity risk for you. In that sense one might even say that the annuity is *more* liquid than a securities-based portfolio.

As for surrender charges, they are inescapable and referring to them as a "penalty fee" can be unfair and misleading. Insurance companies are not in the business of "penalizing" their customers. Your insurer invests your premium in mid- to long-term matching assets. If you walk away too soon you require them to be sold, perhaps at a loss. An annuity's declining surrender charges have a critical economic purpose. They are the gates required by state insurance regulators in order to qualify a policy for sale; they are intended to recapture upfront costs on products that were designed to be held for several years and thereby protect persisting policies from the imposition of extra costs by those who choose to surrender early. The remedy? Be sure not to over-commit to the FIA. Calculate your true liquidity needs in advance and set those funds aside.

Which brings us to the issue of costs and expenses in general. Registered Investment Advisor (RIA) Ken Fisher's key criticism of the variable annuity (VA) focuses on its "nosebleed-level" fees and he has a point: In a VA, the combination of mortality and administration (M&E) charges, sub-account management fees and rider costs can amount to 4% and erode market returns year in and year out. Meanwhile mutual funds too deduct sales charges, management fees and 12b-1 marketing expenses that can add up. An RIA's 1% to 1.5% annual asset management fee can itself seem rather high when compared to the compressed rates charged by ETFs. An insurance company has to get paid, too, and it defrays administrative costs and broker commissions by using its share of the yield paid by its general account. Since its operating costs and management expenses are built into the policy crediting-rate formula, insurers do not separately disclose them. A consensus view is that a well-run insurance company may need the first 2.5% of any general account interest earned to cover all policy and operating expenses and provide its shareholders a profit. The rest should end up in the policyholder's hands.

One valid proviso about FIA investing is not to get enslaved to an anniversary date. Remember that your gains are measured from contract anniversary to contract anniversary and that one-day-a-year vantage point can limit your upside capture potential. I often recommend that an FIA investment should be spread over four quarters—in one or more companies—to diversify potential seasonal effects.

The potential for abnormally low returns over the next twenty or thirty years could make the controversial "bonuses" offered by (fewer and fewer) FIAs even more valuable. Applied to your contract at inception and/or as annual credit enhancements each year, these additions can add up. But they are criticized for having little if any real economic effect other than luring consumers into bad bargains. You must keep in mind that bonuses are never free. Longer surrender periods, higher surrender charges, reduced caps and lowered participation rates may well accompany them. Check to see if they do. Moreover, bonuses are never immediately accessible as cash. But rather than lure and deceive, I believe their intent is to incent and genuinely reward. They are actuarial enhancements that are paid to you, your spouse and possibly your beneficiaries *over time* as you exercise the guaranteed withdrawal benefits. To reap the reward, therefore, you need to put the annuity to its highest and best use as a cash flow generator. Give the annuity the time it needs, they imply, and the actuaries will see to it that its yield pays off.

END NOTES

Preface

1. The Fixed Index Annuity (FIA) is an insurance contract for retirement planning that is designed to provide an income that you (and your spouse) cannot outlive. It comes in a variety of forms, differing in terms of both costs and features. Your advisor should be able to explain the differences, and help you determine if one or more may suit your individual circumstances. Your advisor should also be able to explain the differences between traditional fixed, variable, and fixed indexed annuities. The differences are significant. Annuities are not all alike.

In addition to offering a guaranteed annual interest rate for crediting purposes, an FIA offers you elective participation in the growth of one or more market indexes you may direct it to track. It never invests directly in the underlying securities, so it avoids losses attributable to their volatility; instead, the FIA captures returns by means of derivatives purchased or synthesized by the insurer that replicate the performance of the underlying securities. The intention is that, by using derivatives, FIAs enhance their potential returns when compared to more traditional fixed annuities, without exposing principal to market risk (as does a variable annuity).

By utilizing derivatives to speculate on upside market potential, the FIA aims to credit annual "excess interest" greater than the interest earnings on your principal that are used to buy the options employed in the process. In flat or negative market years, an FIA may credit less or, in the worst case, no interest earnings at all. All index interest reflecting market participation is capped or otherwise limited from year to year by formulae that reflect derivative metrics. Caps and other participation limits are imposed by virtue of the structure and pricing of the derivatives themselves; they are not imposed to advantage the issuing insurer. The insurer seeks to maximize the derivatives' returns to flow through to the policyholder.

In evaluating the FIA's potential role in your retirement portfolio, it is vital to assess whether the possibility of lower average annual returns is a competitive disadvantage, by comparing projected lifelong cash flows from an FIA to what you might realistically generate if you invested directly in a portfolio that combines stocks, bonds and cash and faces an open-ended time horizon reflecting increasingly extended longevity expectations.

Guarantees are backed by the financial strength and claims-paying ability of the issuing insurer. The premium you invest is not a deposit protected by the Federal Deposit Insurance Corporation or any other governmental agency. It's critical to review how insurance guarantees operate, and why the financial industry and its regulators permit them to be made and require them to be honored.

Surrender charges apply if an FIA contract is not held to the end of its "surrender period." Depending on the contract, surrender periods can range from as few as 5 to as many as 20 years from the date of issue. Although most FIAs allow limited "free annual withdrawals" unencumbered by penalties or charges, they are not designed for ready access. In choosing to invest in an FIA, always keep in mind that its highest and best use is for money earmarked to generate long-term retirement cash flows, and not speculative or short-term accumulation. Securities lend themselves better to speculation; cash is the preferred form for truly liquid money.

Withdrawals from an FIA funded with after-tax dollars are taxed as ordinary income to the extent of any gain accumulated in the contract. If held in a qualified account, unless it's a Roth IRA, all withdrawals are taxed as ordinary income. Whether qualified or non-qualified, if withdrawals are taken prior to age 59.5, an additional 10% federal "early withdrawal" tax penalty may apply.

FIAs can be complex, and most consumers (and even some financial advisors) are not well acquainted with them. If sufficiently knowledgeable, your advisor should be able to explain their costs and benefits.

Before investing, it is best practice to perform a detailed review of any fixed index annuity you may be considering—including its features, costs, risks, and operational characteristics—as you would when considering any other financial instrument.

2. Financial derivatives are contracts entered into by counterparties the value of which depends on the return on, or the value of, currencies, securities, commodities, interest rates, reference indices or other financial instruments or benchmarks; derivatives include forwards, options and swaps or combinations thereof. For more details, see the discussion in Chapter 7.

Chapter 2

3. Indices are unmanaged, and investors cannot invest directly in them. Unless otherwise noted, performance of indices does not account for any fees, commissions or other expenses that would be incurred. Returns do not include reinvested dividends.

The Nikkei 225, commonly called the Nikkei, is a price-weighted stock market index for the Tokyo Stock Exchange (TSE). It has been calculated daily by the Nihon Keizai Shimbun (Nikkei) newspaper since 1950, and its components are reviewed once a year.

The Standard & Poor's 500 (S&P 500) is an unmanaged group of securities considered to be representative of the US stock market in general. It is a market-value-weighted index with each stock's weight in the index proportionate to its market value. The components represent some 80% of the entire market's value.

The Dow Jones Industrial Average (DJIA) is a price-weighted average of 30 actively traded "blue chip" stocks, primarily industrials, but also including financials and other service-oriented companies. The components, which change from time to time, represent between 15% and 20% of the market value of NYSE stocks.

Chapter 6

4. Investing involves risk, including in the worst case, a total and permanent loss of your principal. Past performance is no guarantee of future results. Neither asset allocation nor portfolio diversification guarantees a profit or protects against a loss in a declining market. Bonds are subject to interest rate risks. Bond prices generally fall when interest rates rise. The price of equity securities may rise or fall because of changes in the broad market or changes in a company's financial condition, sometimes rapidly or unpredictably. Equity securities are subject to "stock market risk," meaning that stock prices in general may decline over short or extended periods of time. International investing involves a greater degree of risk and increased volatility. Changes in currency exchange rates and differences in accounting and taxation policies outside the US can raise or lower returns. Also, some overseas markets may not be as politically and economically stable as the United States and other nations. For this reason, investments in emerging markets can be more volatile.

5. The projections or other information generated by Monte Carlo analysis tools regarding the likelihood of various investment outcomes are hypothetical in nature. They are based on assumptions that individuals provide, which could prove to be inaccurate over time. Projections, no matter how steeped in historical data, do not reflect actual investment results and are by no means guarantees of future results. In fact, results may vary with each use and over time.

Chapter 7

6. An insurance guaranty association provides protection to insurance policyholders of policies issued by an insurance company that has become insolvent and is no longer able to meet its obligations. All states, the District of Columbia and Puerto Rico have insurance guaranty associations. Insurance companies are required by law to be members of the guaranty association in states in which they are licensed to do business.

The guaranty association's coverage of insurance company insolvencies is funded by post-insolvency assessments of the other guaranty association member companies. These assessments are based on each member's share of premium during the prior three years. However, the assessed insurers are granted—in a majority of states—an offset on state premium taxes as a way to recover, over time, all (or a portion of) the assessment.

The amount of coverage provided by the guaranty association is determined by state statute and differs from state to state. Most states provide the following amounts of coverage (or more), which are specified in the National Association of Insurance Commissioners' (NAIC) Life and Health Insurance Guarantee Association Model Law: $300,000 in life insurance death benefits; $100,000 in net cash surrender or withdrawal values for life insurance; $250,000 in present value of annuity benefits including cash surrender and withdrawal values (payees of structured settlement annuities are also entitled to $250,000 of coverage); $300,000 in long-term care insurance benefits; $300,000 in disability income insurance benefits. In most states, there is an overall cap of $300,000 in total benefits for any one individual with one or multiple policies with the insolvent insurer. Benefits in excess of the above limits may be eligible to be submitted as a priority claim against the failed insurer, through which the policyholder may receive additional payments as the insurer's assets are liquidated.

Chapter 8

7. Purchasing an annuity within a retirement plan that provides tax deferral under sections of the Internal Revenue Code results in no additional tax benefit. An annuity should be used to fund a qualified plan based upon the annuity's features other than tax deferral. All annuity features, risks, limitations, and costs should be considered prior to purchasing an annuity within a tax-qualified retirement plan. Any distributions are subject to ordinary income tax and, if taken prior to age 59.5, a 10% federal penalty for early withdrawal may apply.

8. Annuity contracts can provide long-term streams of income payments based on an annuitant's age and amount of premium applied to the contract. The "life only" annuitization option must be implemented by the annuity contract owner and offers limited or no flexibility after implementation.

9. Annuities are insurance contracts that, depending on the contract, may offer a guaranteed annual interest rate. Contracts have substantial variations in terms, costs of guarantees and features, including withdrawal charges. Product and feature availability may vary by state. Any guarantees offered are backed by the financial strength of the insurance company, not an outside entity. Annuities are not FDIC insured. There is no bank or credit union guarantee. It is not a deposit, nor is it insured by any federal government agency or NCUA/NCUSIF. Investors are cautioned to carefully review an annuity for its features, costs, and risks and as to how its variables are calculated.

10. There is a surrender charge imposed, usually during the first 5 to 10 years that you own a fixed index annuity contract. Bonus annuities may include higher surrender charges, longer surrender charge periods, lower caps, higher spreads, or other restrictions that are not included in similar annuities that don't offer a premium bonus feature.

11. With the purchase of any additional-cost rider, such as the GLWB rider, a contract's values will be reduced by the cost of the rider. This may result in a reduction of principal in any year that the contract does not earn interest or earns interest in an amount less than the rider charge.

12. Annuities come in two types: fixed and variable. With a fixed annuity, the insurance company guarantees both the rate of return and the payout. As its name implies, a variable annuity's rate of return is not stable, but varies with the stock, bond and money market funds that you choose as investment options. There is no guarantee that you will earn any return on your investment, and there is a risk that

you will lose money. Unlike fixed contracts, variable annuities are securities registered with the Securities and Exchange Commission (SEC).

13. *Be sure to consider the investment objectives, risks, charges and expenses carefully before investing in variable annuities. The prospectus, which contains this and other information about the variable annuity contract and the underlying investment options, can be obtained from the insurance company or your financial professional. Be sure to read the prospectus carefully before deciding whether to invest.*

14. The investment return and principal value of the variable annuity are not guaranteed. Variable annuity subaccounts fluctuate with changes in market conditions. The principal may be worth more or less than the original amount invested when an annuity might be surrendered.

Made in the USA
San Bernardino, CA
16 December 2018